ON
SHERMAN'S
TRAIL

D1473956

ON SHERMAN'S TRAIL

The Civil War's
North Carolina
Climax

Jim Wise

Charleston London

History
PRESS

Published by The History Press
Charleston, SC 29403
www.historypress.net

Cover design by Marshall Hudson.

Unless otherwise noted, photos are by the author.

First published 2008

Manufactured in the United Kingdom

ISBN 978.1.59629.357.1

Library of Congress Cataloging-in-Publication Data

Wise, James E., 1949-
On Sherman's trail : the Civil War's North Carolina climax / Jim Wise.
p. cm.
Includes bibliographical references.
ISBN-13: 978-1-59629-357-1 (alk. paper)
1. Sherman's March through the Carolinas. 2. North
Carolina--History--Civil War, 1861-1865--Campaigns. 3. Sherman, William T.
(William Tecumseh), 1820-1891. 4. United States--History--Civil War,
1861-1865--Campaigns. I. Title.
E477.7.W57 2008
973.7'378--dc22
                                    2007046945.

For Aunts Blannie and Eleanor.
Now sainted, never Reconstructed.

Contents

Preface

As best an aging brain recalls, my introduction to William Tecumseh Sherman came at around age three or four, in Wink Vaughn's filling station in Madison, Georgia, when one of my Dad's fishing buddies pointed outside and told me, "General Sherman's army marched right down that street right there."

Not sure just what General Sherman was, and imagining his march as a procession of (Sherman?) tanks, I filed away the information and my formative years' impressions of the War Between the States ("Nothing civil about it," I was told) came from Robert E. Lee biographies (I had a proper Southern upbringing), Fess Parker and Disney's *Great Locomotive Chase* movie and *The Gray Ghost* TV series. At a little later age, there was seeing and reading *Gone With the Wind* during the Civil War Centennial.

And still later, as a Duke University undergraduate in Durham, North Carolina, I made acquaintance of Bennett Place—not yet, in the 1960s, a state historic site but just a quiet park inside a stone wall, with a couple of old cabins and a monument to "Unity." It was a good place to go and toss a football around—you'd always have the place to yourself.

And there was putting on a professional Southerner persona in the presence of collegiate Yankees; a couple of visits to Gettysburg, the second of which permanently alienated our children (then six and four) from battlefield tourism; and the realization that my adopted hometown of Durham owed its prosperity, if not its very existence, to the Civil War's coincidental resolution there.

Still, any sense was a long time coming of how Chickamauga connected with Shiloh with Second Manassas with Fort Sumter with so on with so forth with me. So I trace the genesis of this volume to a hot morning in July 1995, standing on Stagecoach Road in southern Durham at a one-lane bridge over swampy New Hope Creek, and hearing Ernie Dollar tell me, "Right here was the last huzzah."

That "last huzzah" was the last firefight of the Civil War in North Carolina—there, right down there. So first on my roster of acknowledgements and thanks comes Ernie—reenactor, artist, historian and presently head of the Preservation Society of Chapel Hill.

Over the years of being a folklore graduate student under the inimitable Daniel W. Patterson and Charles G. Zug at the University of North Carolina; a hometown journalist with several employers; and, most of all, teaching local and Southern history (with the attendant obligation to know what I'm talking about) at my undergraduate alma mater's Osher Lifelong Learning Institute (née Duke Institute for Learning in Retirement), I've absorbed some notions of the past and the process of history making, and acquired others by deliberate research and brooding. Thanks particularly to Sara Craven and Florence Blakeley, DILR former director and volunteer.

Much appreciation also for the mentoring of Durham architects and history appreciators George Pyne and Frank DePasquale, and members of the staffs and friends of Bennett Place, Duke Homestead and Stagville historic sites and West Point on the Eno and Leigh Farm city parks; and for the underappreciated but outstanding librarians John Ainslie and Lynn Richardson and the North Carolina Collection at the Durham Public Library—which happened to have a wealth of primary source material in original editions on which I have relied for this book.

Thanks also to Gordon Clapp, the New England transplant who founded the North Carolina Civil War Tourism Council in 1994; John Dunlap of the Anson County Historical Society; the Reverend Dr. Howard H. Whitehurst of Laurel Hill Presbyterian Church; Julie Ganis of the outstanding Union and Anson County Civil War Websites; and Kim Cumber of the North Carolina State Archives, for advice, information and invaluable assistance along the way.

As always, greatest appreciation and love for my wife, Babs, the eternally encouraging and patient.

In this book, I have tried to point out the layering of pasts in our landscape—for Sherman's soldiers, the Confederates who resisted them and the civilians who survived them—passed through, and lived in, territories already rich with associations from earlier times and in many cases earlier wars. The town of Sneedsboro (also known as "Sneydsboro") for example, which was established by real estate speculators in the eighteenth century, was already abandoned by the time Civil War soldiers came to cross the Pee Dee River there. Also notable are sites that were important in the Revolution and those with connections to the War of 1812 and even with Bonnie Prince Charlie and the Highland rising of 1745 and its conclusion at Culloden.

There are also the pasts overlaid since 1865—the coming and going of tobacco culture, for example; the movements of populations and whole towns as railroads and new highways came; the continuing succession of "New Souths"; and continuing revisions and reinventions of just what happened, and to whom, and why, between April 1861 and April 1865.

This volume begins with General Sherman at one climactic point in North Carolina, flashes back to bring him there and finishes with his last weeks in the state when events in Virginia put the war's resolution in North Carolina and elsewhere squarely into his hands. It closes with Joseph Johnston's surrender to Sherman at the Bennett farm near Durham's Station. To the extent practical, I have tried to let those who were there narrate and comment on these matters, though as their editor here the choices, arrangement and blame are mine—including the decision to leave spellings, capitalizations and other matters of style as the writers had them.

Sherman left North Carolina a changed state, but almost 175 years since his passage have left it transformed. Open fields have turned back to woods and woods to shopping centers. Elizabeth Allston's "two-room houses" have been replaced by brick ranch styles and double-wide mobile homes. The dirt wagon roads turned muddy sloughs through which the armies trudged have hard surfaces now, and run straighter, if they are still in use at all. The railroads are still here, but they now have multilane highways and oversized trucks to compete with.

Goldsboro, which Union Major Thomas Ward Osborn described as "a little town of 6 or 800," has forty thousand people now and a U.S. Air Force base. A planted traffic island down the middle of Center Street honors the former presence of railroad tracks. Smithfield, where Johnston recollected his forces and his wits, has the Ava Gardner Museum to boast of. Hillsborough shows off its Colonial and Revolutionary pedigrees while becoming a suburb of the Raleigh-Durham "Triangle" and expressing its heritage in an annual "Hog Day."

On another hand, some qualities remain. Rain is still, typically, heavy and dreary in the winter and the trees still bloom in the spring. There still are a few small farms raising corn and cotton, and there are still long stretches of open country to suggest the isolation of crossroad villages in 1865, where news was old if it came at all and anything—anything at all—might be coming or awaiting out on the lonely roads.

This project was conceived as a travel guide and remains an invitation to retrace Sherman's route through North Carolina, because nothing brings pasts to present like seeing and touching and experiencing, if possible, the places, the things and the earth that give canvas and context for the story. It is written to help the reader navigate from point to point along the course of events. The historical background is meant to help the imagination of the twenty-first-century traveler feel some sense of "how-it-must-have-been." The itinerary is a suggestion, and it certainly needn't be taken all at once—it may be more rewarding to use it as a sampler.

The battlegrounds, memorials and museums that mark the Civil War's last weeks may be reached most quickly and easily, for the most part, via major modern highways. Where possible and reasonable, though, this guide recommends back roads—"blue highways" and even country lanes—for getting closer to the reality of those marching soldiers on both sides and the people along the way, waiting for what was going to happen.

For the most part, it is pleasant driving. In my youth, I did a bit of car rallying with my buddy Joe Planck. It is a nonracing competition in which drivers and navigators try to follow a set of route directions designed to throw them off. There was a bumper sticker: "Discover America: Get Lost on a Rally." It was a good idea, and it applies to enjoying history just as well. Just to be on the safe side, though, I strongly advise setting out with a good set of maps.

Chapter One

Goldsboro, March 23

S triding triumphant, the great army looked ridiculous. Some soldiers laughed, some swore, some made futile attempts to form ranks. There went one in a tall silk hat, and another in a lady's sunbonnet. Some had horses, some had donkeys, most were on foot and not too many of them had shoes.

They were part of an army, though, a big one—maybe ninety thousand or so in all—veteran and victorious. In seven weeks, they had marched 425 miles through rain and muck, leaving the enemy's country in a swath of ruin 40 miles wide. Two days before, they had repulsed the best effort of a ragtag force that was the best their enemy could muster to block them. They had accomplished "one of the longest and most important marches made by an organized army in a civilized country," according to their general.

That general was William Tecumseh Sherman, "Cump" to his friends, "Uncle Billy" to his troops and the devil incarnate to generations of Southerners to come.

It was Thursday, March 23, 1865. Sherman's army had reached Goldsboro, North Carolina, a railroad junction town that had been his goal since leaving the Georgia coast on the first of February. South Carolina, the "hellhole of secession," was punished: Columbia, its capital, was burned; Charleston, where Rebels fired their first shot, was surrendered; the countryside, through which Sherman's men passed, was stripped practically bare.

Since the first of March, Union elements had been active in North Carolina. Sherman himself crossed the state line on the eighth, and by that time he had let the army know he wanted this state to feel a lighter touch. To his cavalry commander, Judson Kilpatrick, he wrote:

General William T. Sherman.
Courtesy of the Library of Congress.

Deal as moderately and fairly by North Carolinians as possible, and fan the flame of discord already subsisting between them and their proud cousins of South Carolina.[1]

Major General Henry W. Slocum, commanding Sherman's left wing, echoed his superior's sentiments. From Sneedsboro, North Carolina, on the Pee Dee River just above the South Carolina line, he issued a general order:

All officers and soldiers of this command are reminded that the State of North Carolina was one of the last States that passed the ordinance of secession, and that from the commencement of the war there has been in this State a strong Union party…It should not be assumed that the inhabitants are enemies to our Government, and it is to be hoped that every effort will be made to prevent any wanton destruction of property, or any unkind treatment of citizens.[2]

Nevertheless, the U.S. Army had left a trail of ransacked homes, dead livestock and destitution from Monroe to Goldsboro. Writing from Fayetteville, a correspondent of the *Hillsborough Recorder* reported:

The Yankees arrived on Sunday [March 12] *morning, and have nearly destroyed both town and country…Our house and many others were burned, and every thing destroyed. Even the negroes have been robbed and starved. As to valuables, nothing is safe in their sight.*[3]

Perhaps, then, it was not surprising that the anticipated Union sympathies were yet to be found. Major George W. Nichols, a Sherman aide, wrote that the Northerners were "painfully disappointed…The city of Fayetteville was offensively rebellious."[4]

However destructive their trip or unwelcoming the towns along the way, the army had come through, and coming into Goldsboro in an informal review, it showed the effects and results of seven weeks on the road.

"They are certainly the most ragged and tattered looking soldiers I have ever seen belonging to our Army," artillery Major Thomas W. Osborn wrote in his journal.[5]

It is almost difficult to tell what was the original intention of the uniform. All are very dirty and ragged, and nearly one quarter are in clothes picked up in the country, of all kinds of gray and mud color imaginable.

Nichols observed,

We found food for infinite merriment in the motley crowd of "bummers." These fellows were mounted upon all sorts of animals, and were clad in every description of costume; while many were so scantily dressed that they would hardly have been permitted to proceed up Broadway without interruption. Hundreds of wagons, of patterns not recognized in army regulations, carts, buggies, barouches, hacks, wheel-barrows, all sorts of vehicles, were loaded down with bacon, meal, corn, oats and fodder, all gathered in the rich country.[6]

About the same time, Sherman's Confederate counterpart, General Joseph E. Johnston, was about fifteen miles to the west, outside Smithfield.

"Troops of the Tennessee army have fully disproved slanders that have been published against them," he wrote to his superior, General Robert E. Lee, in Virginia.

The moral effect of these operations has been very beneficial. The spirit of the army is greatly improved and is now excellent. I am informed by persons of high standing that a similar effect is felt in the country.[7]

Johnston must have known he was whistling in the dark. By this time, he was well acquainted with his opponent. The summer before, he had faced Sherman in north Georgia in an attempt to stop the Union advance from Chattanooga to Atlanta. Repeatedly outflanked, Johnston was relieved of command by Confederate President Jefferson Davis. Davis replaced Johnston with General John Bell Hood, who proved to be even less effective. Sherman occupied Atlanta in September. Johnston assumed retirement in Columbia, South Carolina.

Sherman had left an ashen Atlanta in November, marched through Georgia and occupied Savannah, on the coast, in time to offer the city to U.S. President Abraham Lincoln as a Christmas present. Meanwhile, Sherman's superior, Union General Ulysses S. Grant, was in an entrenched standoff with Lee around Richmond and Petersburg, Virginia. Figuring that a decisive defeat of Lee would put an end to the rebellion once and for all, Grant wanted Sherman to put his army on ships, sail north and join him.

Sherman had another idea. Rather than going north by sea, he wanted to go by foot, exacting revenge on South Carolina "as she deserves"[8] and further dispiriting the Confederate home front. Desertions, he knew, were all but decimating Lee's army, as soldiers headed home in response to plaintive letters from suffering and frightened loved ones. A land campaign would also sever more of what few supply lines Lee's Army of Northern Virginia had left.

Grant agreed. Sherman meant to set out in early January, but the heavy rains that would beset his advance almost every step of the way north had the wide Savannah River in a torrent that wrecked a pontoon bridge and led him to delay a month for better weather. Meanwhile, on January 15, a Union force captured the Confederate Fort Fisher, which had guarded the Cape Fear River's mouth in North Carolina and the Wilmington port that had been the blockade runners' last resort.

Sherman finally left Savannah on February 1, with sixty thousand men and twenty-five hundred wagons in several columns that stretched as much as ten miles along several different roads. Two days later, at Hampton Roads, Virginia, a four-hour peace conference between the South and the North came to naught. Meeting scant resistance from the scattered Confederate forces under Lieutenant General William Joseph Hardee—a former West Point superintendent who was recognized by both sides as a master of battlefield tactics—Sherman moved rapidly north toward Lee. Recognizing the threat, Lee, himself just appointed the Confederate commander in chief, summoned Johnston, who had by then removed to Lincolnton, North Carolina, to assemble what troops he could to "drive back Sherman."[9]

After some effective delaying actions, Johnston attacked on March 19 near the village of Bentonville, twenty miles west of Goldsboro. His plan was sound, and his men fought well, but the vastly superior Union numbers

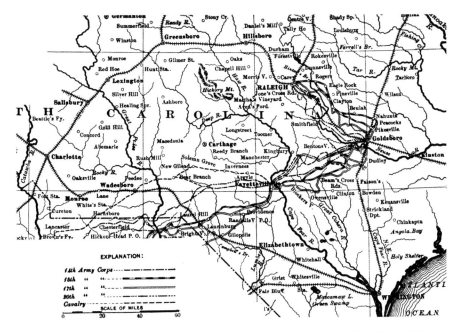

A map of central North Carolina, with the routes of Sherman's corps. *From Osborn,* The Fiery Trail.

proved overwhelming and, under cover of darkness on the night of the twenty-first, he withdrew.[10]

"The Rebels contest every foot of ground with extraordinary pertinacity," wrote Nichols, the Sherman aide, following the Bentonville battle. "More tenaciously than the occasion seems to require."[11]

On the twenty-third, Johnston had less than twenty thousand men left in fighting condition. Some had retreated as far as Chapel Hill, the state university village fifty miles northwest. Some townsfolk met them with whiskey, which was no doubt welcome, but their presence strained resources that were already depleted.

"Some of my neighbors have been constrained to furnish inconvenient supplies of corn, as well as long forage," university president David L. Swain wrote. "We will all breathe more freely when it shall be ascertained that they are all through."[12]

Sick and having found himself left behind during the Bentonville retreat, Confederate Private Arthur P. Ford managed to reach his unit and report to its surgeon.

At eight o'clock on the morning of the 23rd I was driven in an ambulance to a railway station and put with a lot of sick and wounded men on a train for Greensboro. I had had nothing to eat since about noon the day before, and when we got to Raleigh I got off and went to a near-by little cottage, where I saw a woman at the door, and told her that I was really very sick, and very hungry, and begged her for something to eat. I had not a cent of money. She told me pathetically that she had fed nearly all she had to the soldiers, but had a potato pie, and if I could eat that I would be welcome to it. I took it gratefully and it was the nicest potato pie I ever saw.[13]

Near Chapel Hill, in the colonial town of Hillsborough, the war had seemed distant. Local boys were in the fight, but events had stayed far away in Virginia or Georgia or Tennessee. On March 22, the hometown *Recorder's* front page led with a profile of the Russian Field Marshal Suwarrow and a eulogy for the Philadelphia banker Stephen Girard before reporting the reprieve of a condemned Virginian deserter.

Well might the man be spared, for the Confederacy needed every soldier it could hold on to. Each week, the *Recorder* was carrying notices on an inside page:

A last opportunity is offered [deserters] *to wipe out the disgrace and escape the punishment of their crimes…A pardon is announced to such deserters and men improperly absent as shall return to the commands to which they belong within the shortest possible time.*

And:

The discipline and efficiency of the army have been greatly impaired by men leaving their proper commands to join others, in which they find service more agreeable.

Both notices were signed, R.E. Lee, General.[14]

On the twenty-third, Editor Dennis Heartt interviewed a refugee from Sherman's march, a Dr. Glover of Orangeburg, South Carolina. Union troops had taken Glover prisoner before they reached Columbia and held him as far as Lancaster near the North Carolina line. He said that Sherman expressed regret at the burning of Columbia, and that three Yankee soldiers had actually been shot while trying to set fire to houses there. He described the sacking of Winnsboro, South Carolina, and the destruction of fifty miles of the Columbia and South Carolina Railroad, but he had seen no instances of personal violence toward civilians—just that "every man they met on the road was captured and held as a prisoner, unless he could produce evidence that he was not liable to military service."

"The rations of the soldiers appeared to be short," the *Recorder* learned, "and those who were held as prisoners suffered for food—our informant going four or six days without anything to eat."

The newspaper also carried an offer from a Major Gordon, who had "100 bunches of cotton yarn" to swap for "bacon, butter, Irish potatoes, eggs, chickens, etc." Merchant J.Y. Whitted had chewing tobacco, soap and chloroform to sell, and was paying "highest Cash price" for flaxseed. John Cheek was advertising "Mahogany COFFINS of all sizes, at one or two hours' notice."[15]

Still farther west of Sherman's comic marchers, young Elizabeth Waties Allston had traveled through Sherman's trail going up from Society Hill, South Carolina, to her family's plantation Loch Adele near Morven, North Carolina. Years later, she wrote what she recalled:

> *We were never out of the sight of dead things, and the stench was almost unbearable. Dead horses all along the way, and, here and there, a leg or an arm sticking out of a hastily made too-shallow grave. Along the way ten cows dead in one pen, and then eight or ten calves dead in another. Dead hogs everywhere; the effort being to starve the inhabitants out, no living thing was left in a very abundant country. It is a country of small farms, just two-roomed houses; all now tightly shut up, no sign of life.*[16]

Back in Goldsboro, the soldiers were marching—such as it was—in "review." One officer recorded that "nearly every soldier had some token of the march on his bayonet from a pig to a potato." Another called the spectacle "a sorry sight"—victorious or not, heads high or not, they were fighting men in tatters, their bare legs flashing.

"Look at those poor fellows with bare legs," said General Frank Blair.

"Splendid legs! Splendid legs!" said Sherman. "They don't march very well, but they will fight."[17]

For the greatest part, their fighting was all over. Sherman would remain in Goldsboro until April 10. By then, Richmond would be in Union hands and Lee and Grant would have met at Appomattox. For Sherman, the greatest job ahead would be making a peace.

But no one knew that then. On March 23, 1865, Sherman's second great march was complete, but ahead only lay vast uncertainty. In retrospect, it is tempting to see the Confederate defeat as a foregone conclusion to an organic unfolding of events. But that is not the way things happened. When Sherman's men reached North Carolina, there were still battles ahead, many conflicts unresolved and a state that knew something was coming, feared it, but didn't know what it was.

Chapter Two

Moving In

FIRST OF THE YEAR

Museum of the Waxhaws

Approximately 10.2 miles south of Exit 57 on Interstate 485, past the shopping centers and subdivisions down Route 16 to the heart of Waxhaw, North Carolina, then one mile west on Route 75 and right onto a woodsy, winding drive, you reach the Museum of the Waxhaws.

Inside its spacious gallery, past the Siouan Waxhaws, the Scots-Irish settlers, the Revolutionary War and around the Conestoga wagon, there is a section devoted to local son Andrew Jackson—hero of the 1815 Battle of New Orleans and sixth president of the United States. In this section there is a period poster, showing an equestrian statue of Jackson with a rearing steed, and engraved upon the pedestal are the words, "The Federal Union Must Be Preserved."

Ironic placement, for it faces a canvas tent of another era in the area devoted to "The War Between the States."

The tent is about eight by eight feet. It shelters a cot, campstools, chairs and a small table holding candle, bottle and map, and wooden planking for a floor—requisitioned, according to the display card, from the sides of farmers' outbuildings. General Joseph Wheeler, cavalry commander of the Confederate Army of Tennessee, reposes before the tent in a period photograph. The display card reads:

> *February 28, 1865, the Confederate cavalry corps of the Army of Tennessee entered Union County. About 3,000 mounted men commanded by Maj. Gen. Joseph Wheeler spread out across the southern portion of the county. Wheeler established his headquarters at Wilson's Store, present-day Walkersville Presbyterian Church about four miles from Waxhaw.*

The following day in Union County, the war arrived.

The display ranks Wheeler as a major general. According to some sources, he had just been promoted to lieutenant general. According to others, his official rank is unknown but he was exercising the duties of the higher rank.[18] Born in Augusta, Georgia, in 1836, he graduated from West Point, fought American Indians in the West and joined Confederate forces as an artillery officer in 1861. Appointed a cavalry colonel in 1862, he won fame as a raider and distinguished himself by opposing Sherman's advance on Atlanta in 1864.[19]

After the war, he would go into the cotton business and practice law in New Orleans, serve in Congress and reenlist for the Spanish-American War during which his command included Teddy Roosevelt's Rough Riders. But in the winter of 1865, Wheeler's job was to harass the Union advance and find out just what General Sherman had in mind.

Since leaving Savannah, Sherman had played a feinting game—sending units on deceptive moves northwest toward Augusta, Georgia, and northeast toward Charleston, South Carolina, while sending the main force straight north to Columbia. Again, from Columbia, he made a move toward Charlotte, North Carolina, where retreating Confederates were reassembling themselves, to disguise his true intentions in another direction.[20]

By November, when he was still marching to the sea across middle Georgia, Sherman had set a goal of the railroad junction at Goldsboro, North

General Joseph Wheeler. *Courtesy of the Library of Congress.*

Carolina.[21] There he would join forces with General John M. Schofield, who was moving along the line from Wilmington, North Carolina, and General Jacob M. Cox, from New Berne, who was moving along another railroad and the Neuse River. That would create a combined command of about ninety thousand men to march on toward Grant's standoff with Lee in Virginia. In the meantime, he would have wrecked Confederate railroads, further dispirited the Southern civilian population and, just maybe, lured Lee out of his trenches.[22]

All along, Sherman had moved his troops across a wide front, both to avoid clogging the roads and for the sake of deception. It was an effective tactic, keeping his military opponents scattered and the civilians farther ahead wondering whether they were in his path. On Wednesday, March 1, the *Hillsborough Recorder* could only report:

> *For the last eight or ten days we have received very little reliable intelligence of the progress of Sherman in South Carolina, or of the operations of the enemy in any other quarter; what little we get is unfavorable…*
>
> *We stated last week, on the authority of the* Charlotte Democrat, *that intelligence had been received that the enemy occupied Winnsboro, some*

thirty-seven miles this side of Columbia, on Monday [February 20] *and was certainly marching towards Charlotte, General Beauregard falling back. Since then we have no account of Sherman's movements. A gentleman of this town, who left Charlotte on Saturday morning* [February 25], *says that a deep fog seemed to envelop the movement of the enemy and it was not known where Sherman was.*[23]

Before evacuating Winnsboro, Confederate General P.G.T. Beauregard had alerted Lee:

Four corps of enemy are reported advancing on this place…tearing up Charlotte railroad. This indicates his intention not to return by the same route. He will probably be at Charlotte about the 24th…He will doubtless move then on to Greensborough [sic], *Danville and Petersburg.*[24]

Beauregard's estimate of Yankee progress was overly pessimistic. By the twenty-sixth, Wheeler's Union counterpart, Major General Judson Kilpatrick, operating to the north of Sherman's left wing, had just reached Lancaster, South Carolina, twenty-five miles southeast of Charlotte, "having marched through mud and water knee deep to our horses," recalled Colonel Thomas J. Jordan of the Ninth Pennsylvania.[25] At that point, he reported, "The roads are very bad, and the streams much swollen."[26] He had also found the Confederates "strongly picketing" the routes into North Carolina.

Kilpatrick, whom Sherman had described as "a hell of a damned fool," was a flamboyant bantam, a former amateur actor who picked fights as a West Point cadet with secessionist schoolmates. Ambitious (he even had presidential aspirations) and hard driving (one of his nicknames was "Kill Cavalry"), he was also an inveterate womanizer—as his men set fire to the town of Barnwell, South Carolina, in early February, he had invited the town's ladies to a "Nero dance" at one fashionable home.[27] The implicit joke, wrote Union General Smith D. Atkins, "justly stained the reputation of Kilpatrick."[28]

Nonetheless, Sherman had further said that Kilpatrick was just the kind of man he wanted leading his horse soldiers across the Carolinas. Besides his other qualities, he was apparently a cagey fellow, or so considered himself. In a report on the campaign written some weeks later, Kilpatrick states that while en route to Lancaster, he deceived the Rebels for several days with "demonstrations and feints, communications and a well-timed interview with Major General Wheeler,"[29] leaving the Union cavalry free to advance. From Lancaster on February 27, he informed his commander that he was

General Judson H. Kilpatrick.
Courtesy of the U.S. Army Military
History Institute.

holding the roads running in the direction of Charlotte and Monroe.
Wheeler is holding the country in that direction…The enemy are under
the impression that General [J.C.] Davis, Fourteenth Army Corps, is at or
near this point and that our intention is to move upon Charlotte by way of
Monroe. The enemy is now intrenching, to hold the roads in that direction.
I have made demonstrations on all roads in that direction, and have been
met each time by the enemy in strong force…I shall attack if a favorable
opportunity offers.[30]

At the moment, Sherman was about seventeen miles to the south, at Hanging Rock (near present Heath Springs), where a young Andrew Jackson had gained his first combat experience against the British eighty-five years before. He intended to move east, toward the Pee Dee River at Cheraw, South Carolina, as soon as he could. Replying to Kilpatrick, Sherman informed his cavalry commander of Wilmington's capture and predicted that the Confederates, as soon as they realized the Charlotte threat was a trick, would begin amassing an army in North Carolina, near Raleigh.[31]

In the meantime, North Carolinians could hear the war from their homes. Harvey Starnes, then a six-year-old boy living near Wilson's dry goods store in the Jackson community of southern Union County, recalled many years later that his neighbors heard firing at Camp Creek, just below the South Carolina line, on February 26.[32] One of the casualties over the border was Abel Melvin Washington Belk, who was drowned by Union soldiers when he refused to tell them where to find the family's small gold mine. Abel Belk's then young sons, William Henry and John Montgomery Belk, would go on to found the Belk department store company.[33]

Most military-age men of the Jackson community were away in the Waxhaw Jackson Guards, a unit that took 80 percent casualties at Gettysburg—the highest of any unit in the Army of Northern Virginia. But on the afternoon of February 26, soldiers rushed into Union County, up Potter Road to the Wilson's Store crossroads: Confederate cavalry, with Wheeler himself in their lead. According to Starnes, Wheeler ran to the door of a house and informed the residents he would be using one of their rooms for his headquarters, but not to be uneasy. Wheeler's riders spread out across the approaches to Monroe, and artillerymen set up guns on a knoll near the store.

Rain fell again, all day Monday and Tuesday the twenty-seventh and twenty-eighth, but, his men and animals having enjoyed some rest, Kilpatrick left Lancaster on the twenty-eighth and rode nine miles east, toward Chesterfield, South Carolina—stopping for the night at the place "where Tarleton murdered Buford's men during the Revolutionary struggle," as Colonel Jordan put it,[34] and keeping up the feint toward Charlotte as he went along. It wasn't until the following morning, when a scout reached Lancaster to find the enemy gone, that Wheeler realized he was being had.

At 7:20 a.m. Wheeler reported to his superior, Lieutenant General Wade Hampton, "Citizens informed [the scout] that they thought all the enemy had left…Other scouts have been sent forward to ascertain the facts." Later, in the afternoon, he wrote, "The opinion of citizens who conversed with [Union] officers is that the enemy will leave Charlotte to the left. There is talk among the officers that they are going to Goldsborough [*sic*]."[35] Meanwhile, Kilpatrick had troopers roaming north, across the state line, to keep up the trick, while Wheeler's scouts were roaming on their own to see what the Yankees were really up to.

Another display card in the Museum of the Waxhaws reads:

> *Texas Rangers: In Union County, Gen. Wheeler's chief scouts were men of the Eighth Texas, "Terry's Texas Rangers." These were the*

best mounted soldiers in the Confederate army. Texas Rangers kept Gen. Wheeler informed of Union troop movements and found the best roads for the army to march.

WEDNESDAY, MARCH 1

Wilson's Store

"Mar. 1, 1865—Skirmish at Wilson's Store."

"March 1, fought the enemy at Wilson's Store."[36]

Those two cryptic references, the first from a "Summary of the Principal Events" in the *Official Records'* section "Campaign of the Carolinas," the second from Wheeler's own report, are the only direct confirmations of the action that met Wheeler's return from Lancaster. The rest is inferential and tradition.[37]

By the roads, nowadays, it is about eight miles from the Museum of the Waxhaws to the site of Wilson's Store. The fifteen-minute drive also brings a difference in mood and perspective. Where the museum is ordered and enclosed and very up-to-date, the way south becomes natural and open and reminiscent of times past.

Going back out the woodsy, winding drive and toward Waxhaw on N.C. 75, there is a sharp left turn at a three-way intersection at the edge of town. You go toward Cane Creek, on the old Waxhaw-Monroe Road, passing an elementary school on the left, Sims Road on the right and then the octagonal Waxhaw Baptist Church. If you feel adventurous, turn right onto Providence Road and investigate the Jaars Museum of the Alphabet and Mexico Museum (which are just what their names imply). Otherwise, continue to the next right turn and take Bigham Road south, and let yourself decompress. Outlying hints of the Charlotte "Metrolina" spread have fallen behind and ahead are wide, grassy fields undulating off toward tree lines and low ridges. Follow Bigham Road, over a venerable one-lane bridge and through a tight *S* curve, and shortly the road ends at a *T* intersection.

To the left is the tidy brick block of the Walkersville Presbyterian Church; to the right, a homeplace with a healthy stand of cactus; across the road, a low knoll holding the church cemetery; and at the knoll's foot, a rail-fenced enclosure with a brick block beside a pull-off area and a wind-shredded Confederate battle flag.

"Skirmish at Wilson's Store March 1, 1865"

That is all that is inscribed on the stone inset in the brick block. Two black globes suggesting cannonballs top the brickwork. The enclosure is roughly

Wilson's Store site, Union County.

forty by sixty feet, and a couple of cedar trees stand at the far end. There is a sense of wide openness and restful quiet, even when a tractor-trailer rolls by on a highway a few hundred yards away, beyond a cornfield. Here was Wilson's Store. The cemetery knoll served Wheeler as an artillery position and lookout post with a commanding view of the Lancaster Road. Harvey Starnes, who watched the soldiers ride in as a boy, lived almost a century more and now lies buried up there.[38] Potter Road, up which Wheeler had come, now runs a short way east, beyond the church, but it ran past the knoll in 1865.

Union County then was a country of small farms, already suffering in early 1865 from a severe autumn drought as well as the war's privations. Now the armies brought worse. Sherman had yet to issue his directive on going gentler in North Carolina. Whether it would have had much effect or not (whether many of the troops knew which Carolina they were in at this point is questionable anyway), his men did little to win Southern hearts and minds, with long-lasting effect. As Union County historian H. Nelson Walden wrote a century later:

> *The effect of troops, whether Confederate or Federal, was almost the same: devastation. The devastation differed only in degree and intent. Both [sides] were living off the land. The Confederates appropriated supplies*

A plaque marks the site of Wilson's Store, the first skirmish of Sherman's march in North

according to their needs. The Federals appropriated all supplies available and wasted or destroyed what they could not use.[39]

Wheeler, finding the enemy gone from Lancaster and directed to scout ahead,[40] started east, but learned from a scout he met that the Federals were just ahead. Instead of continuing, he turned back north toward Wilson's Store and wrote to Hampton, stating that the cavalry division under General William Y.C. Humes should move that way for lack of forage elsewhere.[41] Arriving back at his headquarters, he found that his troops had been in skirmishes all day across southern Union County and even farther into North Carolina, for Kilpatrick had scouts of his own out looking for his enemy.

From intercepted Confederate dispatches, Kilpatrick learned and wrote to Sherman that the Rebels knew the Union right wing was turning northeastward toward Cheraw and that Southern troops had been ordered out of the port towns of Charleston and Wilmington in order to form a concentrated force opposing the Union advance farther north—even though the Confederates were still unsure just where Sherman was headed.[42] In the same dispatch, Kilpatrick praised his officers: "Learning to be good cavalrymen. All little expeditions sent out have been characterized by that enterprise and dash." For example, the expedition Captain Theo F. Northrop had just led upon the Union County seat of Monroe.

Monroe

From Wilson's Store, Monroe is a twelve-mile drive up busy N.C. 200, a modern Monroe-Lancaster highway that does not appear on Union County maps from the nineteenth century. Kilpatrick's men would have taken a road farther east, probably spotting the courthouse bell tower from some distance away.

Monroe's present-day "Old" Courthouse—built in 1886—occupies the same hilltop as its predecessor, a log structure put up soon after the county was created in 1842 and a county seat established at a central crossroads.[43] On the courthouse square there is the ubiquitous Confederate memorial—an obelisk topped with a sphere—as well as remembrances for other wars and a state historic marker where Marshal Ferdinand Foch, Allied commander in chief of World War I, gave a speech during his U.S. tour in 1921.

One building remains facing on the town square that would have witnessed the Union raid of March 1, 1865: the Old City Hall, a three-story, three-bay, Federal style brick structure across Jefferson Street from the old courthouse. Originally, it was the county jail. The story goes that, in January 1847, a slave ran off from the two-thousand-acre, two-hundred-slave plantation of one John Medlin and was apprehended eight miles away. Medlin and his son-in-law, Clemont B. Curlee, went to bring the slave back—and did so by dragging the man behind their cart. The slave died, and Curlee and Medlin were charged with murder—the local population was so aghast that the case was moved to another county to ensure a fair trial. Curlee was exonerated. Medlin was convicted of manslaughter and would have hanged except for his invocation of an old British law that exempted literate men from execution. Instead, he was fined $3,000 and court costs of $390.39—the money went to building a jail, with quarters upstairs for the county sheriff.[44] Decades later, the town bought it for a city hall.

Now, Monroe is a town of about thirty thousand, part of greater Charlotte with a fast-food, convenience store and shopping center strip running miles along U.S. 74/601 just north of the old courthouse square. In 1865 it was a country crossroads, incorporated just eleven years, but with young elm trees planted and growing all around the public square. According to one account, set down from memory long after the fact, many of the elms were broken when a band of Confederate scouts came to town with a train of seventy-five supply wagons, which they had captured from Union troops

Old City Hall, Monroe, built in 1847 with John Medlin's $3,390.39 fine for killing his slave.

passing to the south. The scouts sold the mules and supplies as quickly as they could and got out of town before any Yankees caught up to them.[45] Yankees arrived at about 3:00 p.m. on March 1.

> *A squad of thirty-five Yankee cavalry dashed into the village of Monroe, Union county, remaining about an hour and left, carrying off all the horses and mules they could gather up. A train of wagons, ten in number, belonging to a party of refugees from Chester District* [South Carolina], *had just reached the village and were standing in the street when the Yankees appeared. Of course the train was seized, and horses, mules, and wagons with their contents, and nineteen negro men, were carried off. Thirteen of them escaped from the enemy and returned to Monroe the same night. The loss is a heavy one to the unfortunate refugees, for we suppose the wagons contained all the valuables they possessed. The women and children that accompanied the wagons were left standing in the streets of Monroe.*
>
> *No buildings were burnt in the village—not even the Court House and Jail were injured—but the enemy seized whatever they wanted and carried it off. Two couriers (sent out from this place) stationed at Monroe, were captured—Charley Brem and Marshall Jones.*[46]

Perhaps Brem and Jones were the sources of some of the information Kilpatrick passed along to Sherman. Kilpatrick was also pleased with the horses and mules Northrop's party brought back to camp, now at Chesterfield, twelve miles west of Sherman. For Union County, the worst was over.

Elsewhere in North Carolina, Hillsborough newspaper readers saw a Northern reaction to the failed peace talks between Union and Confederate representatives. "Old woman talk," wrote a correspondent for the *Cincinnati Commercial*, who complained that the prospect of the war's end had "put a stop in recruiting, buried the coming draft in oblivion, and deprived the army of thousands of volunteers." Cadets from the Hillsborough Military Academy were back in town, reportedly to guard prisoners of war being shipped there for "safe-keeping." Security had been lax:

> *Some Yankee prisoners, officers we understand, arrived here day before yesterday, and by some hook or crook were permitted to take a general stroll about town. Subsequently it was deemed prudent to circumscribe their perambulations.*

The cadets were a cheering presence, the *Recorder* felt: "A good-looking company of lads, and their cheerfulness and spirit reminds us of that exhibited by our volunteers in 1861," but remained, nevertheless, too young for "an arduous and protracted campaign." The paper also reported on the ingenuity of a Confederate physician who had made his way to London to study the manufacture of artificial limbs, bringing along the "truncated members" of several officers, and produced "a number of arms, legs, hands, etc." almost indistinguishable from the originals.

On more somber notes, they could also learn that Wilmington had surrendered and the Union had reoccupied Fort Sumter where the war began.[47] Confederate deserters were terrorizing Randolph County, well north of Sherman's path, prompting Governor Zebulon Vance to direct the home guard there to organize and get to work with "no half-way business."[48] Vance was also getting reports of slaves conspiring "and plotting and persuading other slaves to insurrection";[49] and, from Robert E. Lee, complaints of desertion—several hundred North Carolinians had just walked away from their trenches and gone home, and the general pleaded with the governor to do something to raise spirits on the home front.[50]

THURSDAY–SATURDAY, MARCH 2–4—ANSON COUNTY

Vance's assignment was only made more challenging by nature itself—or citizens' interpretations of it—even before the war broke out.

On January 19, 1861, the northern lights were visible as far south as Wadesboro, North Carolina. Mrs. George Willoughby, working in her garden the next morning, heard a neighbor say the aurora had been "like blood on the earth, and it means that blood will be shed between the North and the South."[51]

Created in 1750, Anson originally reached indefinitely west, a point of some note to local historians, but its territory was quickly partitioned into newer counties as settlers reached, and the colonial government laid its authority upon, the Carolina backcountry. Some of those settlers took issue with that authority through the Regulator movement of the late 1760s and early 1770s, and during the Revolutionary War the county was a place of divided loyalties. Flora McDonald, a Scottish patriot who escorted Bonnie Prince Charlie Stuart to safety on the Isle of Skye after his defeat at the Battle of Culloden, migrated to south-central North Carolina with a great many other Highland Scots and had just bought land in Anson County in 1775. Also like many of those expatriates, she was a Loyalist when the Revolution broke out and, after her husband was captured leading a Tory force to join the British at Wilmington, she escaped the colony and sailed back to Scotland to stay.

By the Civil War, Anson had become a calmer place, a cotton farming region with a handful of industries: among them a tanning works and two small gun factories that, in their modest way (about one rifle and a few bayonets per day), served the Confederate cause. While its sons went off to the army, the county itself figured to be out of harm's way: banks in Fayetteville and Wilmington sent money there for safekeeping, and the Episcopal bishop of North Carolina, Thomas W. Atkinson, relocated there with his family from Wilmington, fearing that the port would shortly fall into Union hands. In that, he was correct; in thinking Wadesboro a safe haven, he proved sadly mistaken.[52]

To Wadesboro from Monroe is a twenty-six mile, forty-five minute drive by way of four-lane and much-developed U.S. 74. There is little, if anything, along it to even hint of the war, Sherman's presence or a history at all. Alternatively, take a back road—a country road, not even a "blue highway"—one of those routes where pavement only overlies the past, where the road is one with the landscape rather than imposed upon it and the dips and twists and curves are felt and a connection with the ground remains, under floorboards and suspension if not quite under foot. Besides, it is a pretty drive.

From Monroe's courthouse square, take State Route 200 to the U.S. 601/74 strip. Go east then bear off on 601. Go past the country club then watch carefully for the left turn onto White Store Road. After the turn comes a veer to the right; then settle in for the ride, continuing on White Store Road through some more pleasantly rolling soybean fields rimmed by hardwoods, through a small range of steep hills, which flatten out at the Edwards community. It is a quiet road—even, it may seem, lonely. Eventually, riding, you may feel you have the countryside, the sky and the hills all to yourself.

By the time you reach the *T* intersection at Lower White Store Road, you are in Anson County. To the right, over a creek and up a hill, is the crossroads of White's Store—prominent on nineteenth-century maps and still occupied by a country store, though "convenience" is a better description now. The Corner Store has a rustic look, caters to deer hunters and is a handy pit stop on the way east. Continue on Union Church Road, which becomes Deep Creek Road, crossing N.C. 109 at the Lowery community and go on toward Cason Old Field, past sandy cotton fields and ranch-style houses set well back from the road.

Long setbacks are a modern convention. In earlier times, the wagon roads—and, before those, footpaths—were the only avenues of communication and no one built more than a few dozen feet away. Out in the country, privacy was plentiful, connections with the rest of the world were more valuable and thus, any farmstead would have been a close and tempting mark for roaming foragers like those who scoured this country in early March 1865.

> *General Hardee had retreated eastward across the Pedee, burning the bridge* [at Cheraw]. *I therefore directed the left wing to march for Sneedsboro', about ten miles above Cheraw, to cross the Pedee there.*[53]

With Kilpatrick's cavalry swarming ahead of Sherman's left and skirmishing almost constantly with Confederate cavalry,[54] about twenty-five members of Anson County's Home Guard, which included Wadesboro *Argus* editor and publisher Frank Darley, assembled and rode out from Wadesboro "in defense of their firesides" to deal with Yankee foragers down toward the South Carolina line. They found "some evidence of the enemy's operations that day—the burning houses upon Seth Jackson's plantation." No sooner had they made camp for the night when their pickets on the White Store Road were fired upon, and they spent the night anticipating another attack.[55]

Sneedsboro

Traveling on from Cason, take the second road to the left along a sandy ridge, past Sandy Ridge Baptist Church, to N.C. 145 and follow that into Morven and U.S. 52. Turning south and passing the New Jerusalem Holiness

Church, you come to a state historic marker, which reads: "Sneedsboro. Laid out 1795, promoted as inland port town on Pee Dee River by Archibald Murphy. Only graveyard remains 5 miles southeast."

For several days, Union troops crossed southern Anson County en route to the Pee Dee crossing. Turn onto the Sneedsboro Road and go east a few miles, and, just when you have been lulled by the passing of woods, and then woods and more woods, around a sharp bend to the right, slow down and watch on the left for a gravel road and two signs:

> *Sneedsboro. Town chartered 1795, second town in Anson County. 1790– 1830. Streets were laid out and named, Methodist and Baptist churches, post office, general store and academy. Land originally owned by William Edgeworth, then purchased and developed by William Johnson. Cemetery is all that remains of the town.*

And:

> *Sneedsboro Cemetery, c. 1790–1840. Follow footpath and signs to cemetery. Neither Carolina Power and Light or Anson County Historical*

Cemetery at Old Sneedsboro, a town established by land speculators in 1795 but abandoned by the time Sherman's left wing arrived to cross the Pee Dee River there in

Society will be responsible in case of accident or injury. Restored by Anson County Historical Society and Carolina Power and Light Company.

The wooden signs are very weather-beaten, and the gravel road becomes twin dirt lanes separated by high grass that lead .3 mile into the pine woods. The cemetery sits just in the middle of the woods, a built-up plot inside a rock retaining wall with chunks of brick fitted in among the larger stones. Some quartz rocks are set out in rows, marking graves, along with a few stone slabs lying flat on the ground:

In Memory of Charles W. Harris who departed this life January 15, 1804 aged 33 years. At an early period his mind was enlightened by the beams of science. His prospects were for higher respectability in life but ah! He fell an early victim to the great destroyer, death.

And, next to him:

In Memory of Robert W. Harris who departed this life June 19, 1812 aged 33 years. He was a tender husband an affectionate father a benevolent friend. A deep sense of religion impressed his mind and colored his actions. Blessed are the dead who die in the lord.

And:

William Johnson born November 3, 1761 married November 9, 1784 to Martha R. Johnson. Died 1840. Revolutionary soldier Virginia and North Carolina NC General Assembly Sneedsboro developer circa 1795–1830.

Besides the cemetery, the only trace of Sneedsboro is a crumbling chimney, isolated in a soybean field a few hundred yards away. In the respectful quiet and solitude, you might reflect that these folk were already long laid to rest and the town they built was already going to rubble and dust when soldiers by the thousands, muddy and wet and fatigued with only more miles ahead, settled in here, coming up a road perhaps much like this cemetery path.

Morven

After you have spent some time reflecting, come back to the twenty-first century and go back the way you came to Morven. The place, originally Covington Tavern on the Charleston-Charlotte stage route, was settled by

Scots in the 1700s and established as a post office under Hugh McKenzie's mastership in 1823 and named for Morven, Scotland, home of McKenzie's mother. By 1865, it had about fifty homes, two bars, a cotton gin, horse races and cockfights on Saturdays. That community was about two miles east of present-day Morven. The town was rebuilt on the now abandoned Cheraw and Salisbury Railroad after raiders burned most of "Old Morven" in 1865. Now, though, like a lot of country crossroads, new Morven itself wears an air of abandonment. About 570 residents remain.[56] U.S. 52 leads up from the sandy flats into red clay country and Wadesboro.

Wadesboro

Early on Friday, March 3, Sherman directed Kilpatrick to reconnoiter well to the north, checking enemy movements and reporting road conditions as well as blocking Confederate dispatch traffic along the plank road toward Wadesboro.[57] Colonel George Spencer of the Union First Alabama Cavalry reported the day's progress as "through a clay country with horrible roads," making camp about three miles into Anson County. No sooner had he set out pickets than they were driven into camp by a Confederate cavalry charge, and, just like the Anson Home Guard the night before, Spencer's unit spent the night expecting another attack.[58] A foraging group from General John Geary's division reached Wadesboro, about fifteen miles north from the Lancaster-Chesterfield road, but Confederate cavalry turned them back.[59]

Other Federals fared better. A tradition in the Bennett family of Anson County tells that soldiers reached Wadesboro and accosted the Bank of Wadesboro's cashier. They made off with his watch and personal valuables, but the bank's own money was hidden at a private home.[60] The home guard returned just about that time.

> *We rode leisurely on back, and had just reached the Court House, where we found a motley crowd of Home Guard, aged citizens, children and negroes, many of them much frightened at a report that the whole of Kilpatrick's command was advancing on the town, and we had just dismounted, when a body of the enemy—some seventy-five or a hundred in number—were seen rising the hill by the Masonic Hall and dashing toward the Court House, yelling and firing at the crowd in front of that building. There were not more than ten of us who had arms in our hands and when the enemy were first seen they could not have been more than a hundred yards from us. A stampede instantly took place by the crowd, and we found ourself standing alone in the middle of the street, bullets whizzing all around us…The party, after dispersing the crowd assembled in front of the Court*

A "bummer." *From Nichols,* The Story of the Great March.

House, soon spread through the principal streets arresting and robbing [citizens] *of their hats, boots, watches and pocketbooks, and stealing all the mules they could lay their hands upon.*[61]

The war caught up with Bishop Atkinson that day. The third bishop of the diocese of North Carolina, Atkinson was commemorated as "the greatest man I have ever known" by his successor, Joseph Blount Cheshire.[62] A Virginian by birth, he was educated at Yale and Hampden-Sydney colleges. He first took up the law and heard a call to ministry in 1836. South Carolina elected him its bishop in 1853; then changed its mind upon discovering his dislike for slavery. It is interesting to note, however, that he twice turned down the bishopric of Indiana because, he said, he would feel uncomfortable among abolitionists. As bishop in North Carolina, he advocated literacy for slaves, founded two schools for white boys and opposed the notion of racial inferiority.[63]

On March 3, 1865, however, he found himself looking into the business end of a pistol. As he described it in a letter to an acquaintance in Chapel Hill:

Some companies of Kilpatrick's cavalry…came on Friday, third March, to Wadesboro, in Anson county, where I was then residing. As their approach was known, many persons thought it best to withdraw from the place before the cavalry entered it; but I determined to remain, as I could not remove my family, and I did not suppose that I would suffer any serious injury. I saw the troops galloping in, and sat down quietly to my books, reading, having asked the other members of my family to remain in a room in the rear of the building. After a time a soldier knocked at the door, which I opened. He at once, with many oaths, demanded my watch, which I refused to give him. He then drew a pistol and presented it at me, and threatened to shoot me immediately if I did not surrender it. I still refused, and, the altercation becoming loud, my wife heard it, ran into the room and earnestly besought me to give it up, which I then did. Having secured this, he demanded money, but as we had none but Confederate, he would not take that. He then proceeded to rifle our trunks and drawers, took some of my clothes from these, and my wife's jewelry; but he would have nothing to do with heavy articles as, fortunately, he had no means of carrying them off. He then left the house, and I went in search of his officers to ask them to compel him to return what he had taken from me. This might seem a hopeless effort; for the same game had been played in every house in the town where there seemed to be any thing worth taking. However, in my case, the officers promised, if I could identify the robber, to compel him to make restitution. The men, accordingly, were drawn up in line, and their commander and I went along it examining their countenances, but my acquaintance was not among them. It turned out that he had gone from my house to that of a neighbor, to carry on the same work, and during my absence had returned to my house, taken a horse from the stable, and then moved off to his camp at some miles' distance.[64]

Kilpatrick settled down for the night on the Wadesboro road, his cavalry guarding roads across the southern part of Anson County, from White's Store just east of the Union County line to the Pee Dee River at Sneedsboro,[65] and resting up for another day's business on March 4.

Early in the day, in compliance with orders from division headquarters, a scouting party of 100 men, under command of Major McBride, was sent to Wadesborough, nine miles, with written instructions to "clean out the town." The major proceeded to Wadesborough, destroyed a grist-mill, saw-mill, tannery, large Government stables and all other public property.[66]

Camped that night at Sneedsboro, General John Geary had had a hard day's traveling. The roads, he wrote, "were of the worst description, the entire surface of the country being quicksand." The country itself he found poor, "yet our foragers brought in abundant supplies, mostly from the regions between us and Wadesborough."[67] Bishop Atkinson had a different perspective on the second day's visitation:

The next day other bands visited us, taking groceries from us and demanding watches and money. They broke open the storehouses in the village; and as at one of these I had some tierces of china and boxes of books, these they knocked to pieces, breaking the china, of course, and scattering the books, but not carrying them off, as they probably did not much value them, and had, fortunately, no wagons. I finally recovered nearly all of them.[68]

Atkinson, though, considered his experience light compared with others in Anson County. Homes of rich and poor were ransacked, corncribs emptied or burned, cotton burned and residents brutalized. "Delicate females had loaded pistols pointed at their heads or breasts with threats of instant death or something worse." James Cottingham and James Bennett were shot dead when they could not hand over valuables that had already been stolen by other bummers.[69]

If mother was living, she could tell better than I can of the hardships and troubles of that cruel war—how hard it was to give up her only son and have to provide for a family of girls alone, and of the raid of Sherman's army, who destroyed the stock of provisions, house and furniture, and left the people to suffer the consequences with the free negroes. I was small, but well do I remember seeing the Yankees riding the roads, with their horses loaded with meat, chickens, blankets and everything they could carry. They burned the mills and gins. I saw Mr. Lockhart's gin burn. It was full of wheat and cotton. I can't tell half what we suffered from the effects of the war.[70]

It was not just Sherman's Yankees leaving ruin, though.

Large bodies of men [—] calling themselves "Wheeler's cavalry," who passed through this section after the main body of that General's command did as also stragglers from other commands and deserters [—] have been almost as destructive to our farmers as the public enemy, in stealing and carrying off horses and mules. Where some of the sufferers from the enemy have been so fortunate as to pick up an old "rip" of a horse or mule left by the Yankees they have had them stolen by some one of these wretches.[71]

Wrote editor Darley, "The heart sickens to look upon and contemplate the ruin they have left behind." However, not all the events of March 3 and 4 in Anson County were acts of inhumanity. Mrs. Willoughby, the Wadesboro gardener, took pity on two Northern boys taken prisoner and confined in town. She baked them cherry pies, for which the boys asked to pay her, and later, when they were back at home, they wrote her their thank-you letters.[72] Their mothers, no doubt, would have been pleased.

Sunday—Wednesday, March 5–8—Richmond County

Wadesboro, like the much larger Monroe, is built around a hilltop courthouse just south of U.S. 74. Calvary Episcopal Church, wreathed by sasanqua camellias, still stands on Wade Street, a few doors east of the eighteenth-century Boggan-Hammond House and its 1839 Alexander Little Wing—both have been restored and are operated as museums by the county Historical Society. The 1820 sanctuary where Bishop Atkinson worshipped, though, was replaced by a new building in 1920. Similarly, the Baptist Church across the street was founded in 1847, but occupies a modern structure.

To follow the Union advance one must, now as in 1865, cross the Pee Dee River, and since the only bridge convenient is the one on U.S. 74, it is time to leave the country roads—which can become tiresome after a while, after all—and head east toward Richmond County and Rockingham, where more travail came to the unfortunate Atkinson. The Federals, he wrote, "in their march through Richmond county, passed by two railroad stations where I had a piano and other furniture, which they destroyed."

Richmond County (which then included the present-day Scotland County) was on edge even before the Yankee approach. Since the war began, white residents of the cotton growing region had worried about a slave uprising and, in December 1864, a report went about that one was indeed brewing, scheduled to break out on Christmas Eve and incited—rumor had it—by deserters and escaped federal prisoners. Investigation uncovered guns and ammunition. "A large number" of slaves were arrested and three were lynched. Nevertheless, the county remained in a state of near panic, with residents demanding action from the governor and the home guard called to duty. December 24 passed without incident, but tension and trouble carried over into the New Year: food prices were astronomical, schools closed, streets were empty and people were "very despondent."[73]

The winter's weather could hardly have helped the popular mood. Cold and rain made life miserable for Union, Confederate and civilian alike, while refugees from South Carolina brought horror stories and retreating Southern soldiers were not only evidence the enemy was closing in, but added strain to what resources the county had left. Strain was wearing on the soldiers, for on March 5, the evangelical General O.O. Howard issued a directive from Sherman's headquarters:

> *The attention of officers and soldiers of this army is called to the gross and criminal practice of profane swearing which prevails and is increasing amongst us, so much so that every sense of good principle and good taste is outraged. Have we forgotten that God is our kind Father and that He is helping us—Every insult to Him is a scourge to ourselves and invites disaster to our noble cause.*[74]

A couple of Sherman's officers, at least, were on their good behavior when they called at a Richmond County home. According to a local story, Mary Ann Covington had awaited the enemy with stern resolve, and one morning just after breakfast one of the house servants announced there were Yankees at the back door. Covington went, and found two Union men on horseback near her steps. They raised their hats and asked, "Madam, could you give us a glass of wine?" Over the servant's protests, Covington sent for a decanter and glasses, but when the officers were served, one asked if she would not taste the wine first.

"No," she said. "If you think I would poison it, just dash it on the ground. You have very little conception of the character of a Southern lady if you think she would poison a gift to an unsuspecting enemy." Reassured, the officers had their drink and departed. Unfortunately, Covington was soon after visited by a crowd of not-so-courteous bummers.[75]

The plundering and skirmishing that had gone on in Anson County carried across the Pee Dee River. Kilpatrick crossed the river during the night of March 6 and the next day—in weather "delightful" for a change, according to one Union report—occupied Rockingham, driving a Confederate cavalry division out of town "after a considerable skirmish, in which the rebel General Aiken was killed."[76] That same day, Sherman sent Kilpatrick orders regarding his behavior in North Carolina:

> *In conversation with people evince a determination to maintain the Union, but treat all other matters as beneath a soldier's notice. Give us a whole country with a Government and leave details to the lawyers. Deal as moderately and fairly by the North Carolinians as possible, and fan the flame of discord already subsisting between them and their proud cousins of South Carolina. There never was much love between them. Touch upon the chivalry of running away, always leaving their families for us to feed and protect, and then on purpose accusing us of all sorts of rudeness.*[77]

Having reached Cheraw himself, Sherman—who despised the press anyway—discovered a New York newspaper that reported he was headed for Goldsboro. "Extremely mischievous," he called it, for now his elaborate deception was exposed to his opponent, whose identity he had also just learned: "Ole Joe" Johnston.[78]

On February 23, Johnston had received a wire from Jefferson Davis, directing him to go see Lee, whom Davis had just appointed the Confederacy's general in chief. Davis probably held his nose as he wrote the order, for he and Johnston had repeatedly clashed throughout the war—most recently in August 1864 when Davis relieved Johnston of command in north Georgia, replacing him with the impetuous John Bell Hood to disastrous results. Much of the South was blaming Davis for the loss of Atlanta and Georgia's devastation, and Johnston himself had gone to Richmond in December in hopes of restoring his reputation and standing with Davis's government.[79]

Johnston, an 1829 West Point graduate and veteran of the Seminole and Mexican wars, had commanded Confederate forces in northern Virginia

General Joseph E. Johnston. *From Johnston, Narrative.*

from the summer of 1861 until he was wounded at the Battle of Seven Pines on the Virginia Peninsula in May 1862. Replaced by his West Point classmate Robert E. Lee, Johnston had had a desk job as nominal supervisor of Braxton Bragg's and John Pemberton's armies in the western theater. After Bragg's humiliation at Chattanooga, though, Johnston took over the Army of Tennessee, and in the spring of 1864, he began his long holding action against Sherman's drive toward Atlanta, fighting a defensive war to minimize casualties he could not afford. That was what had so exasperated Davis.

Lee, though, had a better appreciation of Johnston, with whom he had had a mild rivalry since military academy days. Lee had urged Davis to reappoint Johnston and later, on the same day he got Davis's wire, Johnston received an order from Lee to take command of the Army of Tennessee and all troops in South Carolina, Georgia and Florida, "concentrate all forces and drive back Sherman."[80]

At the time, Johnston was in Lincolnton, North Carolina, a small town at the edge of the mountains that had become a haven for fleeing South Carolinians. Among the refugees was the diarist Mary Boykin Chesnut, who apparently disliked the folk she met there as she recorded them as being dirty and given to spitting tobacco juice without regard for where they were.[81] Johnston's wife, Lydia, whom the general had sent north from Columbia, found them hungry and despondent and the surrounding countryside already stripped of provisions. Johnston had joined his wife in January, while his supporters in Richmond battled Jefferson Davis to get the president to put Johnston back in charge of something. Davis had just finished a painstaking negative critique of Johnston's prior performance when he finally relented.[82]

His morale boosted by Lee's vote of confidence, Johnston went to Charlotte to meet Beauregard, who was technically in charge of the eight thousand or so men facing Sherman under Hardee's direct command. "He assured me that the feeble and precarious condition of his health made the arrangement a very desirable one for him," Johnston wrote.[83] Thus relieved that he was not creating a rival, he proceeded to assess the situation. Besides Hardee, who had been falling back from the Savannah River since Sherman started north, he had about five thousand men under Bragg, who had retreated from Wilmington and settled down at Goldsboro. Men from the Army of Tennessee were drifting east, about two thousand of them were already in Charlotte and about one thousand more were in South Carolina, apart from Hardee. Altogether, they made a potential force of twenty thousand with which to "drive Sherman back."[84]

"We could have no other object," Johnston concluded,

> *in continuing the war, than to obtain fair terms of peace…For the Southern cause must have appeared hopeless then, to all intelligent and dispassionate Southern men…Even if united before the powerful Federal army, the Confederate forces were utterly inadequate to the exploit of driving it back, being less than a fourth its numbers.*

Making matters worse, he had no money to pay what troops he had, and nothing to feed them—all stocks in North Carolina were earmarked for Lee—which meant that Johnston's army would have to forage along the way as they assembled, losing time in the process. Of necessity, then, buying time became Johnston's strategy. Leaving Beauregard in Charlotte to guard the railroad to Virginia, Johnston made his headquarters in Fayetteville—only to learn that Bragg was facing an enemy advance of his own, from Kinston.[85]

Leaving Cheraw on March 6, Sherman entered North Carolina on the eighth near Laurel Hill—east of Rockingham on U.S. 74 and what was then the Wilmington, Charlotte and Rutherford Railroad. General Geary, thwarted four days earlier in his attempt to raid Wadesboro, found the

General P.G.T. Beauregard. *From Nichols,* The Story of the Great March.

General Wade Hampton. *From Johnston*, Narrative.

railroad in good running order. "The structure is excellent, laid with T-rail of the best English make," he wrote, nevertheless destroying three-quarters of a mile of the track and a supply of those good English rails stacked for shipment elsewhere.[86] A few miles to the east, a Federal unit raided Laurinburg, in present Scotland County, and burned the depot and railroad shops that had been relocated from Wilmington before that city fell.[87] Farther east, in Robeson County, an anonymous witness described the "brutal, inhuman and merciless Yankeeism…escaped fiends from the lower regions."[88] In Springfield, though, Lieutenant Colonel Frederick J. Hurlbut attempted to stop a fire.

Soon after entering the town a large fire broke out on Main street, which threatened in its progress to reach the rebel hospitals, four in number, filled with some 500 patients. To prevent this I ordered Major Johnson's command to tear down and remove such buildings as were necessary between the fire and hospitals, thereby saving them, although the greater portion of Main street was burned to the ground. Guards were placed over nearly all the houses in the city and the streets were kept constantly patrolled. Several small fires broke out during the night, but by prompt and energetic efforts, both of officers and men, they were suppressed without material injury. At 2 p.m. Colonel Gillette, of General Howard's staff, called for a detail of two commissioned officers and fifty men and three teams to remove a quantity of gunpowder, cartridges, and shells from a ravine in the northeast part of town, where they had been thrown by the enemy on their evacuation. The detail was furnished, and under the orders of Colonel Gillette cleared the ravine of powder, shells, &c., and were dismissed by Colonel Gillette.

March 6, at 7 a.m. a tremendous explosion took place in the ravine above referred to, which totally destroyed several houses, stampeded a train near by, and killed and wounded a number of soldiers belonging to a command that happened to be passing. On investigation it was ascertained that kegs of powder and shell had been buried by the enemy in the ravine and trains of powder laid therefrom, reaching to the streets in several places, and scattered loose powder around. Just before the explosion a regiment halted in the street and the soldiers, observing the loose powder, began igniting matches and applying them to the powder for amusement. At last one of the trains of powder caught fire and communicated with the buried kegs and shells.[89]

Other fires along the army's forty-mile-wide front were more harrowing. The Union troops had reached the pine forest that stretched from the Pee Dee River to the Cape Fear: homeland of North Carolina's naval stores industry. Sap-rich trees and the innumerable mills making pine rosin, tar and turpentine presented tempting targets for Southern renegades and Northern bummers, and by the time Sherman crossed the state line, the forest, in places, was ablaze. General Edwin Eustace Bryant of the Third Wisconsin described the place:

The black pines along the road had been scraped of their bark by pitch gatherers, to cause pitch to run, and were coated with pitch to the height of seven feet or so. The pitch hung down all about the tree. The troops in passing set these trees on fire by hundreds and thousands along the route. The men were obliged to march, oftentimes where the heat of these burning trees was so intense as to scorch their faces; and the manes and tails of the horses were singed. The air became so dense with smoke that it shut out the sun, so pungent that it stung the tongue and filled the eyes with tears. The air was thick with an oil soot, griming faces and hands to a jet black, very difficult to wash off and impossible to do without soap. At one place a great turpentine distillery was set on fire by the men to see it burn. It was stored with crude turpentine in barrels, the heads of which were knocked in. By the side of the distillery was a huge pile of resin. The match was applied and in a moment a flame roaring like a cataract was leaping high in air. The turpentine ran down the hillside into an adjoining pond, covering its surface. The fire followed the stream of liquid that flowed from the building, and soon spread over the turpentine floating on the pond, emitting a soft, vaporous steam and beautiful blue, almost green-colored flames...

The grandeur of the scene was increased by the dark night, in which the conflagration "burnt a hole." About the corps stood the dark, tall pines in bold relief of yellow green against the inky blackness of the sky. It was a picture that the powerful artist would delight to behold.[90]

Private C.E. Benton, a stretcher-bearer of the 150th New York, found the burning trees an almost spiritual experience.

The endless blue columns swaying with the long, swinging step which became such a marked characteristic of the men who marched down to the sea; in the long bugle peal and rumbling artillery with chafing horses; in the glimmers of muskets and sabers; and all to be heard and seen only by glimpses under the smoke and muffled by the Niagara-like roar of the flames as they licked up turpentine and pitch. Now came rolling back from the depths of the pine forest, the chorus of thousands singing, "John Brown's Body lies a moldering"...at once a prophecy and a fulfillment.[91]

Away from the fires, though, Sherman's aide, Major George Ward Nichols, found the woods idyllic:

To-night we went into camp in a magnificent grove of pines. The roots of the trees are buried in the spindles and burrs which have fallen undisturbed for centuries. The wind sings, or, rather, murmurs—for that is the sound— through the lofty tree-tops, while the air is filled with delicious fragrance. This evening the sun went down behind glowing bars of silver and purple, although now and then its bright rays would stream out, throwing long shadows across this great cathedral floor, transforming tree and bough into columns and arches of glittering gold. As I write, the campfires dance and flare upward; away out in the dark forest, strange, uncouth forms peer out from the shadows; while a distant band of music, mellowed by the distance, rounds in soothing cadences the restful tattoo. Ah! This is not the blood, the carnage, or the suffering of war; it is its delightful romance.[92]

Murdock Morrison's Gun Factory

Laurel Hill is roughly seventeen miles southeast of Rockingham, by way of the U.S. 74 bypass. Leave the four-lane highway there, making a left turn

Major Henry Hitchcock's tent, sketched for his wife by a magazine artist. *From Hitchcock, Marching With Sherman.*

onto N.C. 144 toward Wagram. The town, which boasted a population of five thousand in 2000 and about fifty in 1865, has a business district along the highway and railroad, which quickly falls behind as you go north and, about two miles out of town, reach a bridge with a large pond and old mill to the left and two historic markers to the right. One of the markers commemorates the Richmond Cotton Mill, a water-powered enterprise of Reconstruction vintage. Its machinery is said to have come from a wrecked blockade runner. The other commemorates the gun factory of Murdock Morrison.

Morrison learned gun making from his wife's grandfather, James Buchanan. Another Scottish immigrant, who arrived some time before 1796, Buchanan was well known for the weapons he produced at his gristmill/smithy/gun works on the banks of Gum Swamp. Each rifle was custom-built, from walnut or maple stock to iron muzzle, and Buchanan tested each one at a range of one hundred yards before delivering the guns to his customers. It was a craftsmanlike process, but slow. Around 1840, Morrison came down from the upper end of the county to learn the gun making trade, married Elizabeth Buchanan and, when Buchanan decided to retire, took over the business.

After the Civil War broke out, Morrison took what money he had and, armed with a government contract to turn out twenty-five rifles a week for the Rebel cause, he built a twenty- by fifty-foot gun factory on Beaverdam Creek. With water power and slave labor, Morrison produced not only rifles but bayonets, knives and leather goods and bullets, keeping up his quota right up until Sherman's men arrived with instructions to capture the gun maker. Alerted, Morrison disposed of his components in a millpond and high-tailed it for the swamp. Meanwhile, the soldiers burned his factory and his house, leaving Elizabeth and their two children to walk several miles to spend the night with relatives.[93]

Old Laurel Hill Presbyterian Church

After enjoying the views of the millpond and marsh, drive northeast again on Route 144, or Old Wire Road—so named because it once ran along a telegraph line. Go through one crossroad and over another creek, and watch for a Civil War Trails sign. Turn right after the sign. Ahead, across a cotton field, there is Old Laurel Hill Presbyterian Church, a white frame building with twin doors and a belfry, which, before many of the fields went back to woods, afforded an excellent view of the surrounding country and its roads. Someone going by the initials "RNN" was probably using it as a lookout on March 6, 1865, and he was probably a Confederate sentry, for in the belfry plaster he wrote, "God bless the South and Our Southern girls" along with his initials and the date. He would not have lingered, for another Laurel Hill graffito reads, "The Yankees rode through North Carolina March the 8th 1865." The latter was signed by "Francis M. Cassiday, Co. A, 39th Iowa Inf. Vols."

A number of soldiers' scribblings are kept in a glass case, with handy transcriptions, in Old Laurel Hill's fellowship hall just to the sanctuary's left. If the church is open at the time you stop in, or if you make arrangements ahead of time, visitors are welcome to have a look. Some of the graffiti appear, at first glance, to be just pencil scrawls. Others are barely legible. But others are quite clear even after all these years and some abuse from those who came later—including a visiting Sunday school group that was, according to Pastor Howard H. Whitehurst, inexplicably told, by its chaperones, that it was OK for the kids to write their own graffiti on the belfry walls.

Such treatment, plus the elements' wear and tear inside the open structure, led the church to remove and conserve some of the soldiers' mementos on their original plaster. Old Laurel Hill, though, is a place where pasts are layered upon pasts, from massive timbers from the 1850s to sweethearts' initials from the 1950s. The present church went up in 1856, but the congregation dates to 1797 and tradition holds that the crossroads was a site of preaching from even earlier. At first, the sermons

Laurel Hill Presbyterian Church, Scotland County, where Sherman slept and soldiers

were delivered in Gaelic, for all the Sandhills were—and are—Highlander territory. Gunsmith John Buchanan was one of the founding elders.

Among its early pastors was the Reverend Archibald McQueen, remembered as "one of the ablest, most consecrated and most useful ministers the church has ever had," under whom membership grew to 296—the largest in its history—between 1830 and 1842. McQueen's ministry, however, was cut short. He married his deceased wife's sister, Mary McLeod, violating Presbyterian canons of the time. He was summarily defrocked by the Presbytery of Fayetteville. The rule was later changed, and McQueen's ordination was restored before his death.[94]

This part of what was then Richmond County was cotton plantation land, and a planter named McFarland owned the land all around the church. He encouraged a town to grow at the crossroads, where the coaches passed between New York and New Orleans, according to tradition, and the touring Marquis de Lafayette once stopped off to have a meal. The town was the original Laurel Hill, with a post office by 1822, but after the railroad was laid five miles to the south just before war began between the states, residents and commerce gravitated there, taking Laurel Hill with it but leaving the church behind.[95]

When soldiers' graffiti was removed from the belfry, conservators discovered bricks placed inside the walls—possibly as extra shielding for Civil

Soldiers' graffiti on display in Laurel Hill Church's fellowship hall.

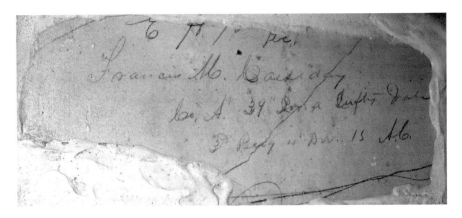

Signature graffito by Francis M. Cassiday, Thirty-ninth Iowa Infantry Volunteers.

War lookouts posted up there. The steeply curving stairway affords a look at the church's monumental framing, and coming back into the sanctuary you find yourself in the old slave gallery, where the original pews remain for use on Sundays and special occasions. The original downstairs pews are gone, taken by Sherman's troops for firewood or to bridge the swollen Jordan Creek just up the road. Someone also made off with the pulpit Bible, but an anonymous Union officer sent another in its place after the war.

After a day's respite on the seventh, the rains resumed on the eighth when Sherman himself crossed the state line and stopped for the night at Laurel Hill Church—sleeping, as best he could (on the march, he sometimes rose after just two hours) on a pew not yet requisitioned. For the first time in a long time he tried to contact the other Union forces in North Carolina. He called in one Corporal Pike and sent him, disguised as a Confederate, to make his way to Wilmington and report Sherman's location and direction to the commander there, confident the city was in Federal hands. He sent a "very clever young sergeant" by a different route with the same message, figuring that at least one would get through. In the message, he asked that a boat be sent up the Cape Fear River to meet him at Fayetteville with bread, sugar and coffee.[96]

Sherman's aide Colonel Nichols found the Charlotte and Raleigh newspapers he picked up along the way quite amusing, with "their lugubrious guesses as to where Sherman will next strike." A journalist before the war, and one who would return to that occupation afterwards, Nichols took careful note of his surroundings once he left South Carolina:

> The soil is not superior to that near Cheraw, but the farmers are a vastly different class of men…The plantation owners work with their own hands, and do not think they degrade themselves thereby. For the first time since

we bade farewell to salt water I have to-day seen an attempt to manure land. The army has passed through thirteen miles or more of splendidly-managed farms; the corn and cotton fields are nicely plowed and furrowed; the fences are in capital order; the barns are well built; the dwelling-houses are cleanly, and there is that air of thrift which shows that the owner takes a personal interest in the management of affairs.

Nichols further observed a difference in the troops' better behavior: "Our men seem to understand that they are entering a state which has suffered for its Union sentiment." He compared the dreary weather to the delights of the day before, concluding, "There is no help for it…I'll to bed, and try to bear it with patience" in a camp he found "still as a grave-yard."[97]

That "grave-yard" stretched for miles along McFarland Road, the soldiers having nearly doubled the county's population by their presence and that of thousands of camp followers, sutlers, refugees and liberated slaves who followed behind the army. Enduring the cold rain and mud, J.M. Lea left his sentiments behind: "O when will this cruel war end and we poor soldiers go home?" Leroy Gamble of Iowa, Hiram D. Jones of Illinois and Thiadore H. Reeve, of unknown origin, just left their names.

The Richmond Temperance and Literary Society

About five miles farther up the Old Wire Road, the men came—and the present traveler comes—upon an odd, squat building tucked well back within a clump of trees. Today, the place is marked by the Civil War Trails, and shares its property with the slightly less aged home of the pastoral poet John Charles McNeill (1874–1907), who is buried in the Spring Hill Cemetery across Arch McLain Road. Take the dirt road past the Trails sign and McNeil house and you come to the hexagonal brick meeting place of the Richmond Temperance and Literary Society.

The temperance movement was established in North Carolina well before the Civil War. The Richmond County group formed in 1853 and soon thereafter had a meeting place constructed of hand-molded, home-fired bricks, near the log cabin founding site of Spring Hill Baptist Church. Gold stars, one for each member, were painted on the ceiling. The stars of the deceased were repainted silver, and if a member fell off the wagon, his star was painted black. Some stars had several coats of paint. The society also gave itself to poetry readings and debate. Atop the roof peak is an oversized carving of a book with a goblet upturned upon it, representing the society's two interests. When Sherman's men came by, they shot the book and goblet down[98] and generally ransacked the interior. It was more than a month before the society could use its hall again, and then it was recorded in the April 22 minutes by secretary J.M. Johnson that:

> *After a considerable interruption, caused by the unwelcome visit of Sherman's thieves, the Society meets again. And, of course, when God's own house is outraged by the Yankee brutes, temples of morality and science will not be respected.*
>
> *We find the ornaments of our fair little hall shattered and ruined; our book shelves empty; the grove strewn with fragments of valuable precious volumes; the speeches and productions of members who are sleeping in silent graves, torn and trampled in the mire, "as pearls before swine."*
>
> *Ye illiterate beasts! Ye children of vice! Ye have not yet demoralized us. Today we marshall our little band again; and with three cheers for Temperance and literature, unfurl our yet triumphant banner to the breeze.*[99]

After some time with Temperance Hall and the adjacent McNeill Gardens, and perhaps a stroll through the old cemetery, drive back down 144 to McNair Mill Road, turn right and go to U.S. 15–501. Make another right, and head north through empty pine forest and roller coaster sand hills toward Aberdeen and the Malcolm Blue Farm.

Temperance Hall, the meeting place of the Richmond Temperance and Literary Society, was ransacked by Union troops.

An upturned goblet on top of a book represents temperance and literature. Tradition holds that Yankee visitors shot down Temperance Hall's rooftop ornament.

On Monday, the sixth, Beauregard in Charlotte had written Hardee in Rockingham:

> *Fayetteville and Raleigh being evidently the objective points of the enemy, General Johnston and myself contemplate a concentration of forces at the first of those points if possible; otherwise, at the latter. You are therefore directed to remove at once, and rapidly, from your present position to Fayetteville, if still practicable; if not, to Raleigh. The ends to be attained by this movement are so momentous—indeed, so vital—to success of operations which have been determined upon, that it is expected you will permit none but insurmountable obstacles to turn you aside from the attempt, except, of course, if General Johnston should see cause, in the existing state of affairs, to change your instructions and give other orders.*

Johnston saw cause, and that same morning he wrote to Hardee that it was too late for a rendezvous at Fayetteville and instructed him to make for Raleigh by the best route he could find. Johnston further wailed, "Where is the cavalry?" Hardee promptly replied that he would come by way of Fayetteville, and cavalry was coming with him. He requested that Johnston have forage and rations ready there for his command.[100] But much of the cavalry was behind Sherman by now—as the Union commander approached Laurel Hill and Kilpatrick ranged east from Rockingham, Wheeler was just getting across the Pee Dee—and to get ahead of him and join Johnston it would be a race, and a fight, at a place called Monroe's Crossroads.

Chapter Three

Fighting Through

WEDNESDAY, MARCH 8—BLUE FARM

Going north toward Aberdeen on U.S. 15–501, you soon discover why this region is called the "Sandhills." For some stretches of the twenty-mile drive, the road affords a roller coaster ride: up and down, up and down and then another steep rise ahead, with flanking pine woods almost unrelieved except for tracts where trees have been cut for timber or pulpwood. Some early chronicles called the region "the Pine Barrens" and even "North Carolina's Desert," for the sand and relative infertility, which led to its twentieth-century development as a patchwork of golf courses.

Highland Scots coming up into the area from the Cape Fear River found the hills covered with longleaf pine, the favored tree for rendering tar, pitch and turpentine, and the bottomlands between them overgrown but, once cleared, adequate for farming. From the 1740s they settled in—John Campbell Blue arrived around 1768. Blue amassed more than eight hundred acres, which were divided among his six sons when he died in 1814. One of them was Malcolm McMillan Blue, who followed his father's example of buying land. His acquisitions eventually totaled almost eight thousand acres, including a tract on the Pee Dee Road (present-day Bethesda Road), where he built a home in 1825 and began a family of his own. He and his wife, neighbor Flora Ray, had seven children.[101] A 7.5-acre tract of Blue's land, including his house, is now owned and operated by the Malcolm Blue Historical Society.

You can reach the Blue Farm via N.C. 5 South—a right turn from U.S. 15–501 just past the U.S. 1 intersection—a wiggly route through the town and into its woodsy suburbs. After a couple of miles, a wrought-iron archway over the road announces Bethesda Cemetery. Go through—yes, through—the cemetery, past Bethesda Church and the farm will be on your left. It is easy to miss, shaded as the house is by century-old oaks. Parking is in a

A Union camp in the longleaf pines—an idyllic spot turned inferno when bummers ignited turpentine works in the Tar Heel State. *From Nichols*, The Story of the Great March.

vacant lot at the corner. In addition to the house, the site holds a windmill, gristmill, several barns and the barn-like Clayton-Blair Museum, which was added in 1986. A remarkably rich and well-interpreted trove of local history, the museum's exhibits cover the turpentine industry, Scottish immigration, pioneer women, home crafts and the War Between the States—in particular, the Battle of Monroe's Crossroads, which took place on March 10, 1865.

Two days earlier, Johnston in Fayetteville had ordered Wade Hampton, then behind and to the left of the Union cavalry, to move and concentrate his command on Sherman's front—which by that time was with difficulty crossing the Lumber River, known in its upper reaches as "Drowning Creek," and driving back the only Confederate force between it and Fayetteville. The ailing Beauregard, in Charlotte, wrote to Johnston suggesting that he and Governor Vance "call on the people residing along Sherman's supposed line of march to remove temporarily all their supplies and animals at least twenty miles to the right or left of his flank routes." Johnston, meanwhile, wired Lee that he still, "after [troop] concentration hope[d] for opportunity to fight his divided troops," but, just in case, he inquired as to where he could cross the Roanoke River in a withdrawal to Virginia.[102]

The barn-like Clayton-Blair History Museum at the Malcolm Blue Farm, Aberdeen, has a detailed display on the Monroe's Crossroads battle.

THURSDAY–FRIDAY, MARCH 9–10 — MONROE'S CROSSROADS, ROCKFISH

As the crow flies, the Fayetteville of 1865 lay about thirty miles east of Blue Farm, where the war arrived on March 9. The museum displays how then ten-year-old Isabelle ("Belle") Blue recalled the visitation:

> *The army was expecting battle because they spent all day in throwing up breastworks. Coming up out of the south, the army came along Pee Dee Road that ran from Raleigh to Cheraw. Soldiers took charge of everything inside. My family was allowed half of the house and they took over the rest. The Yankees began coming at 9 a.m. and kept arriving all day. All the food and provisions were taken over and the Negroes were kept busy all day cooking for the army. The soldiers dug up hams and provisions that had been buried. They then…wreaked general havoc just for devilment. They made white-haired old men ride bareback while they poked fun and played pranks. When the army finally decamped with cannons and cavalry it headed north toward Solomon Grove Post Office* [East Connecticut Avenue in present-day Southern Pines]. *Cleaned out of provisions and supplies, my family had to make a two-day and one-night trip to Fayetteville. Then carpetbaggers molested the horses and stole what they could get away with. The days were dark and gloomy after the war was over.*

"Treasure hunters" dig up a civilian's yard. *From Nichols,* The Story of the Great March.

While that was going on, cavalry commanders were plotting. The day before, Kilpatrick, "making the most difficult march over the most horrible roads, swamps and swollen streams," had caught up with the rear of Hardee's retreating Confederates at Solemn (or Solomon's) Grove, a point on the Morganton Road slightly north and east of Blue Farm. From prisoners, he learned that Hardee was going to Fayetteville and that Hampton was coming fast to catch up. "I determined at once," he wrote later, "to intercept him."[103]

Kilpatrick posted a brigade on the Morganton Road and another on the Yadkin Road three miles north. Scouting himself with several hundred men and some artillery, he made camp at a crossroads to the east and then went scouting again in the evening with an escort of sixteen men and his staff. Hampton, though, with Wheeler and the riders of Major General Matthew C. Butler, had out scouts of his own. One of them had just reported to Butler, having spotted signs of a large body of troops moving just ahead, when Kilpatrick and his band appeared. Butler managed to capture all sixteen of Kilpatrick's men, but the general and his staff got away.[104]

Knowing, then, that Kilpatrick was close, the Confederates reconnoitered under cover of darkness and found Kilpatrick's camp—the general himself was spending the night in the house of one Charles Monroe. Hampton, Butler and Wheeler then devised a wake-up call for their adversary, who had

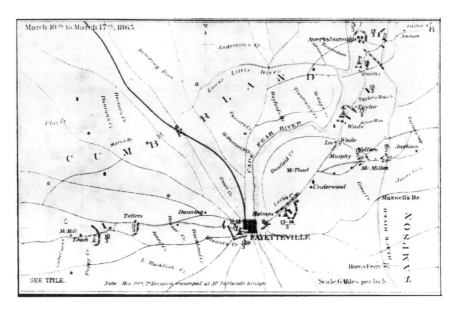

A Civil War–era map of the Fayetteville area. *Courtesy of the North Carolina State Archives.*

for some reason left his own camp unguarded on the north and west sides. Moving men into position through the wee hours, they struck at dawn and caught Kilpatrick with his pants down. Literally.

Moving through dark woods, with the extra cover of fog, the Confederates passed through sleeping Yankees to the very edge of Kilpatrick's camp while, behind them, Hampton told Wheeler to lead his own men and Butler's to make the attack. "We fell upon the camp like a small avalanche, riding pell mell over the enemy, asleep many of them, while others were preparing their coffee," wrote Wiley C. Howard, a lieutenant in the Ninth Georgia Cavalry. Kilpatrick, by some accounts, was inspecting the horses in his slippers. By others, he was shocked awake by the shots and commotion and dashed onto the porch in his nightshirt. By his own account, he fled on foot. By others, he leapt onto a horse and galloped away, barely escaping capture for the second time in less than twelve hours.[105]

Whatever the particulars, Kilpatrick did leave behind his companion of the evening: Marie Boozer, age nineteen, the woman who had accompanied him since Columbia, leaving "a trail of wagging tongues." Reputed to be the most beautiful woman in South Carolina, Boozer came from a family holding Unionist sympathies and made common cause with the Federals when Columbia was in flames.[106] The museum at the Blue Farm displays a poem about her:

Her golden curls bounced,
drawing contempt from heads with tight buns...
Yet her Mother's home on Washington Street went up in flames,
The streets were gutted.
Marie vowed, while rolls of fire shot into the black night,
"From this day, I'll say 'Yes.' 'No' has got me nowhere.
Little Marie will hold the winning hand."
She said "Yes" to four Yankee generals.
When the showdown came, Marie rode out of that burned city
with General Hugh J. Kilpatrick.

Her general having deserted her, the story goes, Boozer came outside in her nightgown. While she was wondering what to do, a chivalrous Confederate rode up and escorted her to the relative safety of a ditch. Meanwhile, Kilpatrick and some troops congregated about five hundred yards away in a swamp Kilpatrick described as "impassable to friend or foe."[107] Wheeler had this to say later:

After a severe fight of some two hours [we] secured some 350 prisoners.
At one time we had the enemy's artillery and wagons in our possession; the
wagons were cut down and the mules driven off. Though we were finally
compelled to withdraw, the attack was a decided success on our part.[108]

Kilpatrick, on the other hand, said this:

The whole command was flying before the most formidable cavalry charge
I ever have witnessed…The enemy, eager for plunder, failed to promptly
follow us up. We rallied and at once advanced upon him. We retook the
cavalry camp, and, encouraged by our success, charged the enemy, who
was endeavoring to harness up the battery horses and plundering my
headquarters. We retook the artillery, turned it upon the enemy about our
headquarters, not twenty steps distant, and finally forced him out of the
camp with great slaughter.[109]

Strangely enough, among the engagement's Union heroes was the First Alabama Cavalry, composed of Union sympathizers who had been hounded from their homes by secessionists and Confederate conscription. Numbers of these men met up in the northeast Alabama mountains, and from there they went to Union lines in Mississippi and Tennessee. The regiment, one of six from the Heart of Dixie to join the Union army and counting both blacks and whites in its numbers, was organized in the fall of 1862 and became part of the Union Army of the Tennessee. When Kilpatrick escaped into the swamp, the First Alabama and Fifth Kentucky came up to support him, and after more than three hours of bloody, sometimes hand-to-hand combat, they prevailed.[110]

Hampton, though, achieved his objective of clearing the Confederate cavalry's way to Fayetteville and linking with Hardee there. They reached the city later on the tenth, some on horseback and some by other means, for Fayetteville had become a hospital town, as described in the following two quotations displayed at the Blue farm:

> *It was on this day that a skirmish was fought at Longstreet* [a church three miles east of Monroe's Crossroads], *12 miles from Fayetteville. Toward the close of day the melancholy line of ambulances came in bearing the wounded and, to me, the still more melancholy file of prisoners. I would have liberated them all if I could, I had not made the acquaintance of Mr. Sherman's bummers then.*
> *—Josephine Bryan Worth, a Fayetteville schoolgirl*

> *About 9 o'clock they had sent for me to come to the hospital and the horrible scene I witnessed there I shall never forget. The wounded had been brought in from Longstreet where a portion of Hardee's men had an engagement with Sherman's men. I stayed with them until just before daylight and did all I could to relieve their wants. Even then I did not hear a single murmur. Such fortitude has no parallel in history.*
> *—Mrs. James Kyle, volunteer matron in one of Fayetteville's hospitals*

Kilpatrick recaptures his camp on March 10, 1865, at Monroe's Crossroads. *Courtesy of the North Carolina State Archives.*

Old Bethesda Presbyterian Church in Aberdeen sheltered Union soldiers before the Battle of Monroe's Crossroads.

The roads Hampton and Kilpatrick's commands traveled, like Monroe's Crossroads itself, are now within the Fort Bragg reservation of the U.S. Army, and as a result of the events of September 11, 2001, they have been off-limits to the public. The Malcolm Blue Farm provides a detailed battle account, along with swords, carbines, ammunition and military hardware characteristic of the battle's time. Back toward Aberdeen on Bethesda Road, the grounds of the old Bethesda Church—also, naturally, Presbyterian—where soldiers camped are a restful place to wander among the tombstones or, as locals are known to do, practice chip shots.

Traveling on now, skirt Fort Bragg to the south on N.C. 211 until you come to Raeford and U.S. 401—a route that approximates Sherman's own path. Take 401 Business through town, then veer right onto Rockfish Road and you will be on Sherman's way to Fayetteville, covering flat, low ground and a series of creeks that, in the torrential rain, gave the Union columns no end of difficulties. High water in the Lumber River caused one unit a day's delay in building a hundred-foot pontoon bridge, which they finished just before a deluge fell. Nichols, Sherman's aide, recorded in his diary that "so large a quantity of rain fell in so short a space of time, that by nightfall the surface of the country was one entire sheet of water." Nichols at that time was about fifteen miles away from his "canvas home" and, even as Hampton was laying his ambush a few miles away, Nichols was having an adventure of his own as he tried, with several couriers, to get back to shelter.

> *The way led through pine forest, where roads, if dependence can be placed in the state maps, existed several years ago. The rain fell in torrents, blinding riders and horses, and drenching every one to the skin…The road soon became less marked; a mile farther it degenerated into a single path; and, finally, it disappeared from sight altogether. Investigations to the right and left and before us gave no clew to the lost track. Halting under the tall pines, we held a council of war…*
>
> *Consulting my pocket-compass, we ascertained that the general direction was correct; yet we hesitated to push blindly through an enemy's country so far in advance of the army, and with so wide a space between the columns, but the darkening sky and sullen thunder warned us to push on in some direction…For miles around nothing was visible but the solemn woods and sandy plains. Another half hour of hard riding ended in another consultation, which had the same conclusion.*
>
> *Some of the party became confused, and insisted we were going north; others thought we were traveling straight toward Fayetteville. There were those who lost faith in the pocket-compass. One or two believed in the little instrument. Every body argued that he was soaked through; no one was cross or discouraged, but, on the contrary, jocose and jolly in spite of the prospect of a night out of doors without food or fire. Most of us had been in precisely that predicament before, and knew very well that the situation would not improve by swearing at it. So we jogged on for a while, and then, gradually looming up in the rain, we descried a blue coat and a white-eared mule approaching.*
>
> *"Halloa, stranger, where are we? Where did you come from, and where are we going?" were the inquiries addressed the new-comer.*
>
> *"Well, I should say that we were in a d----d hard rainstorm…I'm looking for forage in this cussed sand country. Now, where you're going you ought to know best."*

Stumbling upon the forager's camp, Nichols and his companions finally reached their own company around midnight: "rather moist, to be sure, but quite contented that we were not hugging the bark of a pine log away off there in the dark forest." For Nichols, the trouble was that he was ordered back into the woods to ride three more miles, with the encouraging admonitions that "there were holes in the road which were bottomless; that there was no escape by taking to the swamp on either side, for there a man would be drowned." Mounting "a gray nag" named Prince, Nichols observed the horse eyeing him "as if to say, 'I don't like this night trip in the pelting rain, and, besides, I don't know you.'" Traversing a bog and then a lake, guided by the railing of a submerged bridge, he came to a road made a "hopeless abyss" by the army's wagon wheels and an officers' camp where Nichols felt obliged to refuse an evening's hospitality, although Prince was of a different mind. After a few more mudholes and creeks, Nichols reached Sherman—stretched out asleep, for the second night in a row, inside a church.

Some hours later, after having fallen off the horse into the mud as he had just lit his pipe for the ride back to his own camp, Nichols found the way to his own cot. Prince went for a helping of oats and corn.[111]

Rockfish, about six miles past Raeford, has a railroad crossing, a small engine shop and a chiropractic clinic. The name is from Rockfish Creek, a Cape Fear River tributary marked on maps as early as the 1730s, and in 1865 it was home to a 318-loom textile factory, one of the largest in the state, that Northern soldiers burned after wrecking the machinery on March 10.[112]

Sherman recorded the day as one of "some little progress," much of it spent laying wooden planks and tree trunks on the roadways to give horses and wagons, and men, a solid surface to go on. General Giles Smith of the 116th Illinois paused at Rockfish Creek and notified General O.O. Howard, who was commanding Sherman's right wing, that bummers had ventured as close as two or three miles from Fayetteville, where they were told there were no Confederates in the town, and they thought Hardee's Confederate command had already left for Raleigh. Howard replied that Slocum's left wing was to have the honor of going first into Fayetteville, but Smith could move into the suburbs. A bit later, he got an advisory from Sherman telling him that, if he encountered any resistance, he was free to go on and take the city himself.[113]

Sherman might well have been expecting resistance, for prisoners taken at Monroe's Crossroads confirmed that "the whole rebel army is straining every nerve to reach Fayetteville before our forces."[114] To Slocum, he wrote,

> *Do all that is possible to secure the bridge across Cape Fear, but if, as I suppose will be the case, the enemy burn it, effect a lodgment at once across and make a pontoon bridge with a brigade across intrenched. We will await there some days. Destroy nothing till I meet you, unless there be special reason that you know I will approve.*[115]

Hardee's advance troops had reached Fayetteville on Wednesday the eighth, with road crews of "galvanized" Yankee prisoners in the van followed by artillery and infantry, "making an incessant moving panorama of men, horses, cannons and wagons," as the schoolgirl Josephine Bryan Worth wrote in later years. Her family, like others in the genteel river town, opened its home to the soldiers, who streamed through for food, sewing services and a bit of floor to sleep on.[116] Hampton and the cavalry arrived from Monroe's Crossroads on Friday, along with the throngs of wounded and still more infantry.

Whether it was being jingoistic or just trying to alleviate the grim realities of wounded and captive soldiers and the prospect of Sherman's arrival, the *Fayetteville Telegraph* of March 8 had tried to spread some cheer:

> *The prospect brightens. Under the skillful management of Joseph E. Johnston, the campaign is beginning to assume shape and plan and definiteness. The excitement created by the thousand rumors that swept over the land, carrying gloom and despondency to the hearts of our people, has settled into a determination to await with coolness and patience the dispositions of the able officer who has been restored to active duty, and whose sagacious mind now controls, to a great extent, the destinies of North Carolina and the Confederacy.*
>
> *The people are becoming more confident, more hopeful. They feel that there is a man at the helm—one whose coolness and sagacity are sufficient guarantees, that the ship will be guided, with a firm and steady hand, over the breakers, and past the reefs…He has before him the grandest opportunity ever offered for distinction on this continent…the man best qualified to vanquish the pride of the Yankee nation.*

The writer had probably not been privy to Johnston's query to Lee about Roanoke River crossing points. The *Hillsborough Recorder* picked up the story for its next week's edition, running it with the disclaimer, "We hope the editor will not be altogether disappointed in his cheerful anticipations."[117] In fact, when the *Telegraph* came off its press the Yankees were just three days from town, and the general, desperate to pull an army together with any chance of stopping Sherman, had been rather distracted by events to the east and their encouraging result.

> *VICTORY IN NORTH CAROLINA.*
> *One thousand five hundred prisoners captured. The following official dispatch was received yesterday, announcing a victory to our arms in North Carolina:*
> *"Hon. JOHN C~ BRECKINRIDGE,*
> *"Secretary of War:*
> *"General Bragg reports that he attacked the enemy yesterday, four miles in front of Kinston, N.C., and drove him from his position. He disputed the ground obstinately, and took a new line three miles from his first. We*

captured three pieces of artillery and 1,500 prisoners. The number of the enemy's dead and wounded left in the field is large; ours comparatively small. The troops behaved most handsomely, and Major-Generals Hill and Hoke exhibited their accustomed zeal and gallantry.

"R. E. LEE."

Kinston, near which place the fight occurred, is situated on the direct route from Goldsborough to New Berne, and is about twenty miles east of Goldsborough and about thirty from New Berne. It is supposed that this force of the enemy was advancing from New Berne against Goldsborough for the purpose of cutting the railroad at that point. It is not probable after this repulse that the enemy will attempt to advance, and it is likely we shall next hear of them falling back upon New Berne or changing their course to some other point of the compass. This movement of the enemy was evidently designed to be co-operative with Sherman, and in this light and at this juncture it may be of great value to us in embarrassing the movements of Sherman.[118]

Advised that Schofield's Union force was approaching Kinston—a Neuse River town about eighty miles from Fayetteville but just twenty-five from the Goldsboro rail junction—Johnston sent Confederate units from Goldsboro, under command of General Braxton Bragg and reinforced with troops so far assembled at Smithfield, farther up the Neuse, to meet it.[119]

Bragg, to whom most historians give blame for the Confederate disaster at Chattanooga in December 1863 and for whom the present-day Fort Bragg, at Fayetteville, is ironically named, was not on the best of terms with his new superior. In fact, upon learning of Johnston's reinstatement to lead forces in the Carolinas, Bragg had asked Jefferson Davis to be relieved of the embarrassing position as Johnston's subordinate. That was because Bragg, one of Davis's favorites, had been complicit in Johnston's firing the year before. Bragg was instructed to make the best of it and do his job.[120]

Most of the Confederates fighting in North Carolina were from other states—Alabama, Texas, Arkansas—for the state's own recruits had been largely assigned to the Army of Northern Virginia. Indeed, it was a North Carolina regiment that set the Confederacy's "high-water mark" on Cemetery Hill at Gettysburg, and a North Carolinian who fatally wounded Stonewall Jackson by mistake at Chancellorsville. In March 1865 most of those men were entrenched at Petersburg and Richmond as Sherman marched through their home state. But Bragg's command did include some native sons, among them a group under General Robert F. Hoke of Lincolnton that had been withdrawn from the Virginia trenches to help in the defense of Fort Fisher and Wilmington.

Knowing the trouble Lee was having with soldiers deserting to look after their homes, and knowing his own men would be sorely tempted as they rode the trains to Kinston, Hoke had his soldiers transported in boxcars rather than coaches, with guards to discourage anyone from leaving. Even so, men left in droves—only to return to duty within a couple of days.

Hoke also had in his command a squadron of North Carolina Junior Reserves. The twelve hundred youngsters formed the largest brigade in Johnston's army,[121] and they were led by eighteen-year-old Major Walter Clark. "Little Clark," as he was called, was a cadet at the Hillsborough Military Academy when the war broke out and, at fifteen, he joined the army and became a drill sergeant before gaining a first lieutenant's commission in the summer of 1862. He left the service after getting wounded, entered the University of North Carolina, graduated in June 1864 and reenlisted in the Junior Reserves, who promptly elected him a major. Composed of boys who were seventeen and eighteen years old, the Junior Reserves were formed to protect the home front, but as the South's manpower dwindled, the Confederacy was forced to call upon its "seed corn"—as Jefferson Davis had described the Virginia Military Institute cadets who came out to fight in the Shenandoah Valley.[122]

At Kinston, Hoke sent a detachment to flank the Federals and attack from their rear after trudging almost ten miles through a swamp at night. The maneuver paid off, for the surprise attack on the morning of March 8 was a great success. What no one could know at the time was that it was the last victory of any consequence the Confederacy would win in the field, and Bragg's commanders were unable to gain any more ground during the next two days' fighting east of the town at a place called Wyse Forks. After the day's combat on March 10, Bragg called his men back to Smithfield. Nevertheless, the Confederates' early achievement was a tonic in some quarters and it caused the delay of a Union linkup that Johnston needed.[123] On the night of the tenth, Johnston left Fayetteville for Raleigh to coordinate his forces and to figure just where to make his stand.

Elsewhere in the state, accommodating refugees and dealing with lawlessness were worsening problems,[124] yet hope endured. "We have great confidence in the prudence and skill of Gen. Johnston," said the *Hillsborough Recorder*, "and hope that under his management affairs will soon assume a more encouraging aspect."[125]

SATURDAY–TUESDAY, MARCH 11–14—FAYETTEVILLE

The Market House

Past Rockfish, cross into Cumberland County and return to U.S. 401, turning left onto Stoney Point Road and right onto Gillis Hill Road. There are some low hills now, and flat, sandy plateaus with church steeples rising above the treetops before you enter the Fayetteville suburbs. The highway brings you into town, where the Airborne and Special Operations Museum at the corner of Bragg Boulevard and Hay Street is well worth a stop-off out of 1865. Looking east up Hay Street, you will see the landmark Market House—a distinctive building from 1832 with a colonnaded, open ground floor surmounted by a smaller, enclosed second story and a four-faced clock tower surrounded by a traffic circle. Park, stroll along the gentrified Hay Street—an avenue of antique-looking streetlamps, cobblestones and trees once notorious for its GI bars—and come into the old market for a spell.

Standing at the intersection of five main plank roads leading into town, the Market House was a center for commerce. The upper floor served as municipal offices after fire destroyed the Old Town Hall, where the North Carolina Convention of 1789 ratified the U.S. Constitution and the state legislature chartered the state university that same year. Inside the arcade, four stone benches flank a seal set into the brick floor, commemorating the two settlements Campbellton and Cross Creek that were combined to create Fayetteville. A tablet on the wall, placed there by the North Carolina Society of the Colonial Dames of America, displays the history here.

> First organized settlement on the Cape Fear, at the mouth of Cross Creek, 1739; Establishment of Cumberland County, 1754; Incorporation of the town of Campbellton, 1762; Settlement of Cross Creek village, 1765; Liberty Point Declaration of Independence, June 20, 1775; Cross Creek and Campbellton united and incorporated as Fayetteville, 1783; here Lafayette was welcomed, March 4, 1831.

Another plaque commemorates another history:

> "We shall come up slowly and painfully perhaps, but we shall win our way."—Charles Waddell Chesnutt, 1858–1932. In memory and honor of those indomitable people who were stripped of their dignity when sold as slaves at this place. Their courage in that time is a proud heritage of all times. They endured the past so the future could be won for freedom and justice. Their suffering and shame afforded the opportunity for future

Union advance troops exchange fire with Confederate defenders at the Fayetteville Market House. *Courtesy of the North Carolina State Archives.*

generations to be responsible citizens free to live, work and worship in the pursuit of the blessings of liberty to ourselves and our posterity.—City of Fayetteville, 1989.

On March 11, 1865, the Market House was the scene of a skirmish as Federal scouts tangled with rear elements of Hampton's cavalry. Josephine Bryan Worth, the schoolgirl who had felt such sympathy for the line of prisoners, recorded her memory of that morning:

The first intimation that we had that the Federals were really in town was by a jet-black negro mounted on a clay-bank horse. He had lost his hat and his blanket was streaming behind him; he was urging his horse to its utmost speed; his eyes looked as if they would pop out of his head with fright, and at every bound he ejaculated, "Yankees! Yankees!"

A few horsemen followed him, firing their pistols, as they retreated, at some Yankee cavalrymen that appeared above the brow of the hill.—I shall never forget my feelings at the sight of the latter as my aunt said solemnly, "Children, they are Yankees." It was like a knell of doom.[126]

The bummers' arrival actually interrupted Wade Hampton's breakfast, while his fellow cavalry officer, Butler, was sleeping while his clothing was being laundered. Making the best of an awkward situation, Hampton collected seven men and repulsed the bummers, while Butler and his aide, Lieutenant Thornton Tayloe, dashed out of town in what little clothing they could grab, along with the ragged rest of Hampton's cavalry. One trooper stopped at young Josephine's house and asked for a hat, his own having been long lost. Another, on foot, dashed through the yard, shedding arms and gear as he went. As more Federals entered the town, Confederates began firing on them with artillery placed on the Cape Fear River's far bank, "the shot passing through the houses of Fayetteville," while other Southern troops set fire to the only bridge, which had been well doused with pine resin. While the last Confederates retreated, Fayetteville's mayor surrendered the town to the Union.[127]

Fayetteville had grown on a natural terrace about a mile west of the river, and extended from the central crossroads back to the fashionable suburbs on the Hill, just outside the city limits. Eliza Tillinghast Stinson, a longtime citizen, described the Fayetteville of the 1860s as a town without fine public buildings and extravagant homes, but one where the people

> lived well...and took things slow and easy...They preferred plain comfort and the education of their children to that feverish striving after display, often with very slender backing, which is so characteristic of to-day in our feverish railroad towns.

The Arsenal

At the crest of the Hill, the U.S. Army had built an arsenal in 1838 as part of a fortification effort begun after the War of 1812 had revealed how vulnerable the country was to invasion. Fayetteville was a good location because it was on a navigable river and major roads and because it was roughly midway between arsenals at Washington and Augusta, Georgia. The arsenal was regarded as the handsomest building in town, made of cream-painted brick with sturdy walls and towers at each corner enclosing its shops and official residences and a park-like campus where residents liked to take out-of-town guests to impress them with the view.[128]

In 1861, the Confederacy took over the arsenal without incident. In 1865, Sherman made it his headquarters, finding it "in fine order, and…much enlarged by the Confederate authorities, who never dreamed that an invading army would reach it from the west." He further found that the ordinance officer in charge of the arsenal, who had fled with the other Confederates, was the son of his own first captain.[129] He met another old army acquaintance, Edward Monagan, at the arsenal as well. However, after the initial delight at seeing him, Sherman turned grim and rebuked Monagan for turning traitor to his country and to Sherman himself. His staff was shocked by the general's emotion.[130]

The arsenal was a favorite picnic spot for Fayetteville townsfolk. *Courtesy of the North Carolina State Archives.*

Sherman had spent much of his military career in the South, and those in Fayetteville were not the first former friends he had encountered along his march. A native Ohioan, he was first impressed with Southerners and their values at West Point, and he went on to serve postings in Florida, South Carolina and Louisiana. When word of South Carolina's secession reached him, he was superintendent of the academy that is now Louisiana State University. Yet, a sign in his office read, "The Union—Esta Perpetua," and he promptly resigned, stating that he would remain loyal to the Constitution.[131]

Taking time for his engineers to lay pontoon bridges, Sherman could let his men have a few days' welcome break from marching. The weather turned beautiful, and some soldiers took time to enjoy "this beautiful and important place,"[132] which reminded one officer of "some of the old towns in the vicinity of Paris."[133] Some used the time to reflect on what they had accomplished. For Major Thomas Ward Osborn, the campaign had been

> *a very pleasant one…We have marched about 400 miles, destroyed about 200 miles of railroad and all the factories of three large manufacturing cities, Columbia, Cheraw and Fayetteville, where supplies were produced for the southern armies…The enemy has been miserably commanded since we have been on this campaign or we should not have gotten through so easily.*[134]

General Sherman met an old
acquaintance in Fayetteville.
From Johnston's Narrative.

General Henry Hitchcock took the opportunity to write to his wife:

> *We have had rains, sometimes very long and heavy rains, for more than*
> *half the time since* [leaving Savannah]. *This has not been "a holiday*
> *march." The roads have been far worse than anything we saw in Georgia,*
> *and this has involved immense labor and much delay, to say nothing of the*
> *inevitable exposure of our columns, inviting flank attacks which the rebels*
> *have not made. Many miles of "corduroy" roads had to be made, and then*
> *re-made, day after day.*

He went on to describe how the rain dripped into his tent, but he
admitted that the privates had it worse, trying to sleep in their sodden little
"dog tents" and then rising only to labor on "the horrible roads…Yet they
are as cheerful and gay as boys, full of unquenchable spirit, ready to march
again at daylight, ready to fight."[135]

Marching had been equally hard on the Confederates, who were racing
to get ahead of Sherman in time to meet him head-on. Arthur Peronneau
Ford, a private among the troops formerly stationed at Charleston, wrote,

"This march across the Carolinas was a very hard one." Feet became blistered, many soldiers were barefoot, and the winter was a cold one:

> *It seemed to us that it rained and froze constantly.*
>
> *We would march all day, often in more or less rain, and at nightfall halt, and bivouac in the bushes, with every particle of food or clothing saturated. Within a few minutes after a halt, even under a steady rain, fires would be burning and quickly extend through the bivouac. If a civilian should attempt to kindle a fire with soaked wood under a steady rain, he would find his patience sorely tried, but the soldiers seemed to have no trouble.*
>
> *After the fires were kindled we had to wait for the arrival of the commissary wagons; and it was not uncommon for a detail of men to be sent back in the night to help push the wagons through the mud; weary, footsore, hungry, in the dark, up to the knees in mud, heaving on the wheels of a stalled wagon! It was often late at night before the wagons were got up and rations could be obtained…When the rations were drawn they consisted of only seven ounces of bacon and one pint of cornmeal to the man per day; and on several occasions even these could not be had, and the men went to sleep supperless, and with nothing to eat during the next day.*

Not surprisingly, desertions plagued the army along the way north, and the Citadel cadets among them left at the state line. But Ford was cheered by the man who led them, Hardee, nicknamed "Old Reliable," whom Ford regarded as "one of the ablest corps commanders in the Confederate service." He and some comrades managed, while passing through Fayetteville, to equip themselves with new Enfield rifles, "one of the best guns of the day of its kind, and fairly accurate at 600 yards."[136]

Museum of the Cape Fear

Leaving the Market House, take Hay Street west toward the Hill, crossing Bragg Boulevard and going up into, now as then, a residential neighborhood. Watch on the left for the sign for the Museum of the Cape Fear. Turn left and continue for a couple of blocks to the museum, which will be on your right—a modernistic block of a building, with brick and sand-colored panels that suggest stonework, and a flanking tower perhaps meant to replicate some part of the arsenal's own form. Stop and stay a while. The museum, a branch of the state history museum in Raleigh, opened in 1988 and has exhibits on southeastern North Carolina Native Americans, settlement, plank roads, steamboats and slavery, and a hallway devoted to the Civil War.

Fayetteville Market House, the former place of slave sales, on gentrified Hay Street. Nearby, North Carolina ratified the U.S. Constitution in 1789.

There is a Union musician's sword, carbine and musket, cap boxes, bugle, a Union kepi and a weathered valise; and, from the civilian side, a walking cane, lard lamp and sewing machine of the era, as well as quotations.

"Ah, mother, you all at home peacefully do not know the misery of being driven from home."—Sarah Chaffee Lamb.

Not surprisingly, most of the display pertains to the arsenal, and includes a portrait of its architect, William Bell, who rather resembles the Lincoln assassin John Wilkes Booth. A Scotsman trained in Edinburgh, according to the accompanying text, Bell had worked at the College of Charleston and the Citadel before coming to Fayetteville, bringing with him a national reputation for military design. There are cannonballs, an 1863 Enfield musket claimed to be accurate to one thousand yards, swords

Foundation remains in Arsenal Park, Fayetteville.

and flags. The arsenal itself lies just behind the museum and across a footbridge over the Martin Luther King freeway; that is, what is left of the arsenal.

For Sherman, much as he admired the "magnificent" place, tore it down. "We cannot afford to leave detachments" to guard it, he wrote to U.S. Grant, "and I shall therefore destroy this valuable arsenal, so the enemy shall not have its use; and the United States should never again confide such valuable property to a people who have betrayed a trust."[137]

> *Early Monday morning—the third day after he entered the place—we saw a large body of men, seemingly armed with a new kind of weapon, coming from the Arsenal. On closer inspection we saw that each had a fragment of the ornamental wood-work that surrounded the building to make their fires with. Soon the work of breaking down the walls began. Bars of railroad iron were suspended by chains from timbers set up in the shape of an X; with these they battered down the walls, pecking first a small hole which grew larger as they swung the iron against them. There were several such rams at work simultaneously around the same building.*
>
> *When the walls were sufficiently weakened the roof would fall in with a loud crash, the bands would strike up and the men would cheer as if they really enjoyed the work of destruction.*[138]

Crossing over to Arsenal Park, as the grounds are called, you can't help but be struck by the scale—four and a half acres, open space with scattered trees and, in springtime, wildflowers in the grass inside and around the old foundations. Stonework outlines a four-bay rectangular space that reaches south toward the next street and suggests that the building originally extended east into what is now the freeway cut. The first bay, a sign informs, was the Engine House, power plant for the smithy and gun carriage factories. Next is the woodworking shop that turned out gun carriages, wagons and wheels. At the end there is a round foundation: the Southwest Tower, "last of the original four Arsenal towers to be built. In the original plans, this tower was to be the guard and prison rooms." The stones are dark gray, almost black, and are grown over with lichen and weeds in the cracks. Back to the north, there is an anomalous presence marking the site of the northwest tower—a skeletal framework of metal called the "Ghost Tower," whose history is explained on a faded signboard:

The "Ghost Tower" in Arsenal Park marks the spot and scale of the arsenal's northwest tower.

The northwest tower was the first of the arsenal's four towers to be built, 1839–1840. This tower was not scheduled to be constructed before the others, originally planned as a privy. The decision to build the northwest tower first and use it as the facility's temporary office was made by the arsenal's commanding officer, Capt. James A.J. Bradford. The change in building schedule, as with so many other aspects of the arsenal's construction, was the basis of "lively correspondence" between Captain Bradford and his superiors in the U.S. Army's ordinance department. The towers were the arsenal's most prominent features. These three-story, octagonal structures protruded beyond the corners of the square. This architectural style was really a defensive feature. The towers' protrusion allowed flanking fire along the facility's exterior wall. This Ghost Tower is a semblance of the original brick tower and allows visitors to understand the scale of these structures. A steel, rather than a reconstructed tower, was built because of the lack of detailed plans and the scarcity of original building materials.

Again, the scale is impressive.

The arsenal was far from the only Fayetteville establishment to fall at Sherman's hand. Even though the city was a hotbed of secessionist sentiment,[139] Sherman directed his generals to deal "generously" with it as long as the Cape Fear Bridge remained intact and his men met no "positive resistance" upon entering.[140] With both conditions unmet, the Yankees went on a spree—as described by a correspondent to the *Recorder*:

No description can convey a just idea of [the occupation's] horrors. The enemy occupied Fayetteville on Saturday the 11th. About four in the afternoon three Yankees rode up to this house, demanded the keys, loaded their horses with turkeys, biscuits, butter, hams, flour, sugar, &c. They ran up stairs, gave a hurried search through our trunks for jewelry (which was all baubles) and rode off. On Sunday, about five, troops of them came, ransacked the houses and every out-building, burned the factory, warehouses, two hundred bales of cotton, 6,000 barrels of rosin, great deal of turpentine, drew off the waters of the pond, knocked in the heads of the barrels of vinegar and tallow hidden there, found all the meat and molasses (thirty-five barrels), which had been secreted, took all the corn, flour, in short, every mouthful of anything edible.

The editor vouched for the correspondent's reliability, for

from accumulated testimony we are forced to believe that, in burning houses, plundering and robbing peaceful citizens…destroying private property, and in disregard for the feelings of defenseless individuals, they have displayed a fiendish disposition, which has no example in modern warfare in any civilized country—such as only savages can be guilty of.[141]

Railroad property, all the gristmills but one, the Bank of Fayetteville and the offices of the *Observer* and *Telegraph* newspapers, as well as that of the *North Carolina Presbyterian*, were destroyed, in some cases while Union officers looked on as they enjoyed wine pilfered from local cellars. A few gentlemen were robbed on the streets at gunpoint and left, in public, divested of footwear and pants, but the bummers' early looting of private homes in town declined after guards were posted and the brass imposed a degree of order. Things were much worse outside the town core, with glows in the nighttime sky from burning houses in the country.[142]

Outside the town, where no guards were placed, the soldiers "ran amuck" through everything. At my uncle's place, four miles from here, they tore up, smashed and stole everything they could lay their hands on; they cut up the parlor carpet into saddle cloths, broke the mirror over the mantel, broke up the clock and the sewing machine, carried off the books from the library, even the family Bible was not sacred; one of them opened it and spread it over a mule's back and rode off on it for a saddle. Finally they finished by tearing up clothing, pamphlets, feather-beds, &c., and pouring peanut oil over the debris. All the bed-clothes were carried off, except one quilt on which the baby was lying…I wish to confine myself to my own experience and that of my family, or I might multiply instances like these of the conduct of Sherman's men near Fayetteville, such as hanging men to make them produce their valuables, pouring molasses in pianos, converting bureau-drawers into feed boxes, tying up silk dresses for flour bags, and so on; verily the Yankees are an inventive nation.[143]

Rest and recreation were fine, but probably nothing more raised the Union soldiers' spirits than when, on Sunday morning, a tugboat whistle blew from the river. The messengers Sherman dispatched from Laurel Hill had gotten through, and Wilmington had replied.

It was the first courier from the outside world since the army left Beaufort [South Carolina], *nearly two months before. It spoke no word; but the bright, familiar bunting at its peak seemed to be a personal message to every member of the grand army, telling him the Government at Washington yet lived, and the great heart of the nation confided in his patriotism and courage.*[144]

Sherman himself felt the thrill:

> *Soon a shout, long and continuous, was raised down by the river, which spread farther and farther…The effect was electric, and no one can realize the feeling unless, like us, he has been for months cut off from all communication with friends.*

The boat, though, brought none of the supplies Sherman had requested—only dispatches for Sherman's attention. He got to work, writing Secretary of War E.M. Stanton, Grant and General Terry at Wilmington—instructing the latter to send him "all the shoes, stockings, drawers, sugar, coffee, and flour, you can spare."[145]

Besides official reports, requests and orders, Sherman took time to write to his wife, Ellen.

> *I have no doubt you have all been uneasy on our account, but barring bad weather & mud we have had no trouble. I fear the people along our Road will have nothing left wherewith to Support an hostile army, but as I told them their sons & brothers had better Stay at home to take Care of the females instead of running about the Country playing soldiers…I think we are bringing matters to an issue.*[146]

He also used the occasion of reestablished communication to divest himself of "twenty to thirty thousand useless mouths"—the refugees who had gathered to his army—and send them down the river out of his way. Among those who took their leave at Fayetteville was Kilpatrick's paramour, Marie Boozer, who made her way north to more adventures among military men and eventually married a noble European. Most of the refugees, though, had come along "in search of 'white wheat bread and a dollar a day,'" as F.Y. Hedley of the Thirty-Second Illinois put it in his memoir *Marching Through Georgia.*

> *The white refugees and freedmen traveled together in the column, and made a comical procession. They had the worst possible horses and mules, and every kind of vehicle, while their costuming was something beyond description. Here was a cumbersome, old-fashioned family carriage, very dilapidated, yet bearing traces of gilt and filagree, suggesting that it had been a very stylish affair fifty years before. On the drivers seat was perched an aged patriarch in coarse plantation breeches, with a sky-blue, brass-buttoned coat, very much out of repair, and his gray grizzled wool topped off with an old-fashioned silk hat. By his side rode mater-*

Camp-following refugees such as these added to the difficulty of Sherman's advance. At Fayetteville, he sent them away. *From Nichols,* The Story of the Great March.

> *familias, wearing a scoop-shovel bonnet resplendent with faded ribbons and flowers of every color of the rainbow; a silk or satin dress of great antiquity, and coarse brogans on her feet…Those who traveled on foot, men and women, of all colors from light mulatto to coal black, loaded down with bedding, clothing and provisions, were legion. Occasionally a wagon was occupied by white refugees, who, being unionists, had been despoiled by the confederates. These were sad and hopeless. The colored people, on the contrary, were invariably gay hearted, regarding their exodus as a pleasure trip.*[147]

Sherman remained in Fayetteville until Tuesday the fourteenth, collecting and distributing what supplies Wilmington could send him. When the army pulled out, it left a destitute town behind. That day, a resident wrote to his father in Chapel Hill,

> *We are in the greatest distress…There will not be left more than fifty head of four-footed beasts in the county and not enough provisions to last ten days. Many, very many families have not a mouthful to eat…Do spread the word of our destitution, and urge the people to bring us something to eat. If relief does not come many must starve to death.*[148]

Cross Creek Cemetery

Now it is time for the twenty-first century traveler to leave Fayetteville to its fate, but not without one last stop: drive down the Hill, turn left on Bragg Boulevard and then right onto Grove Street, going through town and watching very carefully for Cool Spring Street on the left. Turn onto Cool Spring, cross Cross Creek and climb the hill to Cross Creek Cemetery on your right—it is marked with a Civil War Trails sign. Turn into the cemetery and drive forward until you spot an obelisk with a few flanking headstones. It is the oldest Confederate memorial in North Carolina, erected December 30, 1868:

> *Nor shall your glory be forgot*
> *while Fame her record keeps*
> *or honor points the hallowed spot*
> *where valor proudly sleeps.*

The cemetery dates to 1785. The monument and Confederate graves occupy a hillside that drops sharply down to the creek, which is now overgrown but could be seen when Annie Kyle, the hospital nurse, and

Cross Creek Cemetery, Fayetteville—the first Confederate monument erected in North Carolina, December 30, 1868.

Mayor Archibald McLain established a Confederate burial ground soon after Sherman's departure. According to the Civil War Trails text, the Reverend Joseph C. Huske of Saint John's Episcopal Church officiated at a mass burial there in the spring of 1865 and, after the war, Kyle and other women raised money for a memorial by raffling a quilt. William Bell, the arsenal architect, is in Cross Creek, too. He died in 1867, never, it is said, having recovered from seeing his great work leveled.

Across the street, another Trails sign marks the parade ground of the Fayetteville Independent Light Infantry, North Carolina's oldest military unit and the second oldest militia organization in the United States. It was the unit that seized the arsenal in 1861, and its soldiers, with hats bedecked with plumes from the hats of Fayetteville ladies, went off to war and stayed until their enlistments were up. That's what the sign says, anyway.

Now go on back to Grove Street and away from downtown, turning north on U.S. 301, passing the inviting Cape Fear Botanical Garden and crossing the Cape Fear with considerably more ease than Sherman's soldiers. In years gone by, before Interstate 95 came through, 301 was a two-lane main-line between New York and Florida. There remain a few relics of that yesteryear—mom and pop motels, for the most part—but more emblems of the more recent rural past and the rural present such as shotgun houses and pre–World War II bungalows, double-wide mobile homes and modest modern residences speckling the flat, low country of blackwater creeks and pine trees. After a little while, turn left onto N.C. 82 and continue north, toward the Averasboro Battlefield.

Wednesday–Thursday, March 15–16—Averasboro

From Fayetteville, Sherman's route is a well marked and interpreted trail. Having come up through the bucolic counties along the South Carolina border, it has reached a section of major highways and population centers, where first local history buffs and later, local organizations, the state of North Carolina and the Virginia headquartered Civil War Trails project have located, preserved and developed sites of significance for the benefit of posterity and the convenience of the traveling public. As you go north on N.C. 82, Burnett Road, an example comes up suddenly, on the left, across from the intersection of Ross West Road: two brick blocks bearing large metal plaques, set at an angle like the pages of a book and held open by an attentive oak. There is a sandy pull-off area at the edge of a broad, open field and a brick bench runs between the "pages," inviting a rest or a read.

This monument was placed by the state highway and archives departments and the "Confederate Centennial Commission" in 1961. One plaque recounts the events that led the armies to this place. The other, with a helpful map, explains what happened:

> *You are standing at the center of the first phase of fighting at the Battle of Averasboro…Gen. H.J. Kilpatrick's cavalry division was in the lead, skirmishing with Gen. Joseph Wheeler's Confederate cavalry which contested the Union advance. At 3 p.m.* [March 15] *the Union forces struck a heavy Confederate skirmish line. Gen. Smith Atkins' Ninth Michigan Cavalry drove the skirmishers back into the first of three lines of breastworks erected across the road. The Union cavalry then constructed heavy barricades in front of the Confederate works. At 6 p.m., Confederate Gen. W.B. Taliaferro…ordered an attack.*

Sherman, leaving Fayetteville, figured that Johnston was gathering between forty and forty-five thousand men and meant to strike—somewhere. The Union commander hoped to avoid a fight until after reaching Goldsboro and linking with Schofield and Terry. He wrote to Schofield,

> *with my present force, and with yours and Terry's added we can go wherever we can live. We can live where the people do, and if anybody has*

"Heroes who are not gazetted"—some of Sherman's four-footed troopers. *From Nichols,* The Story of the Great March.

to suffer let them suffer. Collect all the forage you can at New Berne, also provisions and clothing. We will need an immense supply of clothing, for we have been working from knee to waist deep in water for 400 miles and our men will need reclothing throughout.[149]

To keep Johnston guessing just where to gather his forces, Sherman split his command even more than usual and decreased strength on his wings while sending the main body of his army, with its supply train, on the most direct road to Goldsboro. He sent the right wing, under Howard, well to the south, toward Clinton, along a route roughly corresponding to the present-day N.C. 24. The left wing, with Kilpatrick in advance and Sherman himself in the rear, went north toward Raleigh along the Cape Fear River, where it came to a narrow neck between the Cape Fear on the left and the Black River on the right. It was a good place for a surprise, and Hardee's Confederates were waiting.

Johnston's potential force was, in fact, much fewer than what Sherman had estimated, and, as of the fifteenth, it was still in the process of assembling. Although he had Beauregard's advice that Sherman was going to Goldsboro, Johnston had not made up his own mind. To buy time and get information, he ordered Hardee to watch the Fayetteville-Raleigh road while he pulled the rest of his command together at Smithfield, a Neuse River town about midway between Goldsboro and the capital.[150] Hardee was then near Averasboro—usually spelled "Averysboro" at the time—a small Cape Fear River community. He set three lines to intercept the Federals, the farthest about five miles south of the town in an area called "Smithville" or "Smith's Mill," in recognition of the family that had owned plantations there since the mid-1700s.

On the morning of March 15, one of Hardee's advance units, a brigade commanded by Colonel Alfred Moore Rhett of South Carolina, was posted just north of the spot where the open-book monument now stands—near the home of John Smith, "Oak Grove," and a road leading to the Cape Fear ferry that Smith operated. To the south and Rhett's left, just a couple hundred yards from the present monument, was the plantation home of William Turner Smith. This home also stands, and is occupied, to the present day—a fourteen-room Federal period dwelling built in 1835, with a two-story Greek Revival portico. Farther north stands a third Smith plantation, "Lebanon," which is still occupied by Smith descendants.

In midafternoon, the rains having resumed, Kilpatrick's cavalry encountered the Confederates' skirmishers about one hundred yards south of their first line of improvised fortifications. At that point, the Federals came under artillery fire and fell back. Kilpatrick sent word back

Confederate soldiers chase a rabbit that wandered into their camp. *Courtesy of the North Carolina State Archives.*

to Slocum for reinforcements. Firing continued until dark with neither side gaining an advantage, although the Union did take one prize—Colonel Rhett himself.[151]

In deference to the colonel's rank, he was escorted back to the cooper shop where Sherman himself had taken refuge from the elements. Sherman was impressed with the prisoner, describing him as "a tall, slender, and handsome young man, dressed in the most approved rebel uniform, with high jack-boots beautifully stitched." For his part, Rhett was "dreadfully mortified" to find himself in enemy hands, and to have been taken without a fight—he had mistaken some Union troops, inside his own line, for his own men—which Sherman and his officers found highly amusing.

From Rhett, Sherman learned that the Confederates' forward lines were manned by inexperienced troops, which previously had been garrisoned at Charleston, and the general determined to ram through them the following day then turn the wing east toward his real goal. For the evening, he invited Rhett to dine, "and our conversation was full and quite interesting."[152] Major Hitchcock took a rather dimmer view of the captive; a specimen, he wrote, of a polished exterior laid over "devilish incarnate selfishness," boastful about his own untested abilities and the sort of military discipline he believed in.

> *"Conscripts are just as good as any other soldiers; discipline's the thing; all you have to do is to establish the principle. Why, I've shot twelve*

men myself in the last six weeks and not long ago I took a pack of dogs and went into the swamps and in three days I caught twenty-eight men with them."

I have given you almost the exact, literal words he used. This "chivalrous" Southern gentleman; this devil in human shape, who is but a type of his class, and whose polished manners and easy assurance made only more hideous to me the utterly heartless and selfish ambition and pride of class which gave tone to his whole discourse.[153]

After supper, Rhett was passed on to the care of his guards. Meanwhile, reinforcements were hastening from the rear, among them the Third Wisconsin, whose adjutant Edwin Bryant recorded that his men got the order to advance as they were bedding down in a cemetery:

In less than two minutes the brigade was on the road. The night was the blackness of darkness, and the road, a by-road evidently, was soon bottomless. There were no torches, and, as the negroes would say, "de rain done po' down." Floundering on, mud knee deep, with occasional improvement by wading waist-deep in mud and water, the brigade got over five miles. Men had their shoes sucked off by that mud…some stumbled and lost their guns and were thankful that they were not trampled under by the on-moving column and buried alive.[154]

Well to the south, Howard's columns were having difficulties of their own. After a small skirmish, Lieutenant Matthew H. Jamison and his fellows in E Company, Tenth Illinois, encountered a

wide and deep swamp…rebels attempted to burn bridge; failed; we were across about as soon as they—torrents of rain on us all evening. Nightfall—distant cannonading—"Old German Louis" frying flap-jacks in the rain.[155]

On the Raleigh road, fighting resumed on the morning of March 16, with the Union attempting to flank the Confederate line, which was held by the unit Rhett had left behind, while sending another force in direct attack. As Hardee had expected, the untested Charlestonians fell back to the second Confederate line, leaving behind them cannons, which the Yankees quickly put to their own use. With Kilpatrick attempting another flanking, the Federals made another advance in the early afternoon, flushing the Confederates again.[156]

Chicora Cemetery, Averasboro Battlefield, with restored slave cabin from Lebanon

People who lived near old Smithville and the now abandoned Averasboro retained the battle's memory and passed it on, though the battleground itself went back to agriculture and, as time went along, some of the district's historic buildings fell into disrepair. In 1994, local citizens created the Averasboro Battlefield Commission "to identify, acquire, and provide means of preservation" for historic sites in the area, research and publish information on the battle and develop the area's tourism potential.[157] Since then, it has set up a visitors' center, restored the Chicora Civil War Cemetery, bought land and preservation easements, installed monuments, built a battle diorama and had the site added to the National Register of Historic Places. It has plans to turn one of the Smith homes into a transportation museum.

Some of the commission's work is visible as you go north on Burnett Road. There are stone monuments marking the Confederate First Line and then, after crossing into Harnett County and passing the Second Line mark, you'll see the tidy Chicora Cemetery with an 1824 slave cabin the commission restored and moved from one of the Smith plantations and another brick wall from the 1961 centennial with a plaque describing the battle's "Phase II."

A ladies' group, the Smithfield Memorial Association, established Chicora Cemetery in 1872, "In memory of our Confederate dead who fell upon that day," as attested by a marker. A monument reads, on one side, "The hearts that were true to their country and God shall report at the grand reveille," and, on another, "Dulce et decorum est pro patria mori." Fifty-six soldiers are interred there, many beneath stones reading only "Six Georgia men," "Nine Dead," "Six South Carolina Men," "Four Dead," "Six Dead" and so on. The corn and soybean fields stretch out, absolutely flat, to faraway tree lines, much as they did back then. Farther on up the road—which is laid upon the route of the plank road of 1865—is the commission's visitors' center and its museum, a well-appointed facility with artifacts and detailed maps and displays on the Smith family, one of whom left an account of the battle from her own point of view. On April 12, eighteen-year-old Janie Smith, who lived in the northern plantation, Lebanon, wrote to her friend Janie Robeson. The letter is titled "Where Home Used to be."

We would have been better prepared for the thieves but had to spend the day before our troops left in a ravine as the battle was fought so near the house, so we lost a whole days hiding. I can't help laughing, though the recollection is so painful when I think of that day. Imagine us all and Uncle John's family trudging through the rain and mud down to a ravine near the river, each one with a shawl, blanket and basket of provisions. The battle commenced on the 15th of March at Uncle John's. The family were ordered from home, stayed in the trenches all day when late in the evening they came to us, wet, muddy and hungry. Their house was penetrated by a great many shells and balls, but was not burned and the Yankees used it for a hospital, they spared it, but everything was taken and the furniture destroyed. The girls did not have a change of clothing. The Yankees drove us from two lines of fortifications that day, but with heavy loss, while ours was light. That night we fell back to the cross roads, if you remember where that is, about one sixth of a mile from here, there our men became desperate and at day-light on the sixteenth the firing was terrific. The infirmary was here and oh it makes me shudder when I think of the awful sights I witnessed that morning. Ambulance after ambulance drove up with our wounded.

One half of the house was prepared for the soldiers, but owing to the close proximity of the enemy they only sent in the sick, but every barn and out house was fill and under every shed and tree the tables were carried for amputating the limbs. I just felt like my heart would break when I would see our brave men rushing into the battle and then coming back so mangled.

The scene beggars description, the blood lay in puddles in the grove, the groans of the dying and the complaints of those undergoing amputation was horrible, the painful impression has seared my very heart. I can never forget it. We were kept busy making and rolling bandages and sending nourishment to the sick and wounded until orders came to leave home. Then was my trial, leaving our poor suffering soldiers when I could have been relieving them some. As we passed the wounded going to the woods they would beseech us not to go. "Ladies, don't leave your home, we won't let the enemy fire upon you." But orders from headquarters must be obeyed and to the woods we went. I never expected to see the dear old homestead again, but thank heaven, I am living comfortably in it again.

It was about nine o'clock when the courier [sic] came with orders. The firing continued incessantly up and down the lines all day, when about five in the evening the enemy flanked our right, where we were sent for protection, and the firing was right over us. We could hear the commands and groans and shrieks of the wounded...

You inquired after Cam. I believe the excitement cured her. She is better now than she has been for years.

Their house is ruined with the blood of the Yankee wounded. Only two rooms left, Aunt Mary's and the little one joining, which the family occupied. The others she can't pretend to use. Every piece of bed furniture, etc. is gone. The scamps left our piano, used Aunt Mary's for an amputation table.

The Yanks left fifty of our wounded at Uncle John's whom we have been busy nursing. All that were able have gone to their homes, and the others except four, are dead. The poor things were left there suffering and hungry with only one doctor. I felt my poverty keenly when I went down there and couldn't even give them a piece of bread. But, however, Pa had the scattering corn picked up and ground, which we divided with them, and as soon as the Country around learned their condition, delicacies of all kinds were sent in. I can dress amputated limbs now and do most anything in the way of nursing the wounded soldiers. We have had nurses and surgeons from Raleigh for a week or two. I am really attached to the patients of the hospital and feel so sad and lonely now that so many have left and died. My favorite, a little black eyed boy with the whitest brow and thick curls falling on it, died last Sunday, but the Lord has taken him to a better land. He was the only son of his widowed mother. I have his ring and a lock of his hair to send her as soon as I can get an opportunity. It is so sad to receive the dying messages and tokens for the loved ones at home...All nature is gay and beautiful, but every Southern breeze is loaded with a terrible scent from the battle field, which renders my home very disagreeable at times.[158]

The entire letter runs more than twenty-five hundred words. A copy is on display in the Averasboro museum. The North, which referred to the action as the "Battle of Black River," took about 680 casualties and the South suffered about 500 killed and wounded whom it could not replace.[159] On the night of the sixteenth, Hardee pulled his men back, having accomplished two of Johnston's purposes. From prisoners, they knew Sherman was going to Goldsboro; Confederates had had more time to reach Smithfield; and Sherman's two wings were far apart—the right having advanced while the left was delayed. That was what the Confederate commander wanted, and Sherman had no idea. The Union commander resumed his progress as planned.

For all the Southern accounts of Yankee depredations, the Northerners encountered cases of Rebel inhumanity. As the troops moved on Goldsboro, a Captain Duncan appeared, coatless and barefoot. He had been captured in the early skirmishing at Fayetteville, and he told Sherman that Wade Hampton's men had deprived him of his hat, coat and shoes as their general looked on and ignored Duncan's appeal for aid. Sherman sent Duncan on to Kilpatrick's care and later heard that, tit for tat, Kilpatrick retaliated by forcing the unlucky Confederate Rhett to make the trip to Goldsboro on foot. "Of course," Sherman stated in his memoirs, "I know nothing of this personally."[160]

Friday–Tuesday, March 17–21 — Bentonville

Having absorbed what Averasboro Battlefield has to offer, track Sherman north again on N.C. 82, bearing right whenever a sign points the way to U.S. 301. Cross 301 on Arrowhead Road, very close to I-95, and, if you like, stop for a reorientation at the Civil War Trails kiosk just off the Southeast Transformer Co.'s driveway.

After the delay at Smithville, Hardee withdrew east into Johnston County, joining the rest of Johnston's newly christened "Army of the South." Sherman, still with the left wing, crossed the Black River a mile west of 301 and turned east, departing on the night of March 18 to join Howard on the right, "supposing that all danger was over."[161]

In the meantime, Johnston received advisories on the seventeenth and eighteenth that Sherman's objective was, indeed, Goldsboro. At last convinced, he ordered all his generals to converge on Bentonville, a hamlet about twenty miles west of Goldsboro and fifteen miles south of Smithfield toward which, his scouts reported, Sherman's left was moving.[162] All told, Johnston had summoned only about twenty thousand men—half what Sherman had guessed—but with Sherman's wings, Johnston figured, a good day's march apart, he hoped to smash one before it could be reinforced and then turn upon the other. In fact, one of Howard's columns was only six miles from Slocum as Johnston put his men into a *V*-shaped line across the Goldsboro road two miles south of Bentonville and sent Hampton to stall

General Robert Hoke.
*Courtesy of the North Carolina
State Archives.*

the enemy and convey the idea that there were only mounted skirmishers ahead. During the night of the eighteenth, harassed Federals came upon a number of turpentine stills, which naturally they set on fire—thus informing the Confederates of their positions.[163]

Coincidences were on Johnston's side as March 19 dawned clear and sunny. Slocum mistook the skirmishing on his front for the Confederates simply making nuisances of themselves, and he believed the erroneous report of an escaped Federal prisoner that Johnston was concentrated at Raleigh. Kilpatrick, by some uncharacteristically bad scouting, conveyed the same error to Sherman, who had convinced himself that Johnston posed no immediate threat. So, he thought little about the cannon fire he heard from Slocum's direction, and it came as quite a surprise to him when, in the afternoon, a courier informed him "that near Bentonsville General Slocum had run up against *Johnston's whole army*."[164] The italics are the general's own.

Sticking to the secondary roads and countryside, take 301 into the edge of Dunn, then turn east on N.C. 55, drive under Interstate 95 and back into cotton field country. Go through Draughon Crossroads, named, according to a state historic marker, "for George and Hardy Draughon, brothers who came from Edgecombe County about 1795, purchased land adjoining both roads." In about six more miles, N.C. 55 crosses Interstate 40 and comes into Newton Grove. Go around the traffic circle to U.S. 701 and follow the signs to Bentonville Battlefield State Historic Site. The visitors' center there has an animated fiber-optic map that plays a six-minute sound-and-light account of the battle. The onsite Harper House, which served as a field hospital from March 19 to March 21, 1865, is restored and interpreted. A quarter-mile walking trail behind a restored earthwork leads to a surviving line of Federal trenches, and a driving tour leads to marked points where the fighting took important turns then and bungalows and ranch-style homes now guard the restful open country.

A tour marker reads:

> *Main Confederate Line: On March 19, the line extended ¾ mile to the rear of this marker and one mile to the left, forming a strong hook-shaped position with a right-angled turn here…Earthworks remain.*

The nineteenth was a day of twists and surprises. The 104th Illinois, having "proceeded leisurely along for some three or four miles toward Bentonsville [*sic*]" began meeting a little resistance and one trooper had just spied what he thought was a Rebel battery when a cannonball whistled past him and "heavy lines of rebel skirmishers opened up in front."[165] Another Union

Restored earthworks at Bentonville Battlefield historic site.

brigade, discovering Confederate breastworks blocking its way, attempted to flank the breastworks only to encounter "a fire that had another sound than that of carbines."[166]

For the Confederate Private Arthur P. Ford, the day was memorable for more than combat. Having gone without socks for a month and his shoes falling apart, Ford nevertheless tried to keep his feet healthy by frequent bathing. Rushing toward Bentonville to join the fight, he paused at a stream for a quick soak when General Hardee himself appeared and berated Ford for straggling. Ford, though, leapt to attention, put on a contrite face and explained what he was doing, whereupon the general saluted, begged his pardon and rode on.

The rest of his day was more serious as Ford and his companions passed wounded men heading for the rear and improvised operating tables where surgeons were busy and piles of amputated limbs already littered the ground. The wounded included a great many Northern men, for the Confederates had just overrun their position. They begged the Confederates for water, which was freely given, and one Southerner, attending a Yank with a crushed leg, produced a flask of whiskey and offered it to the suffering man. The Federal accepted with gratitude, saying, "Thank God, Johnnie; it may come around that I may be able to do you a kindness, and I'll never forget this drink of liquor."[167]

Initially, the Confederates gained the upper hand that day, driving one Federal division from the field, and as late as 11:00 a.m., two hours after fighting began, Slocum was still so sure he faced only a minor impediment that he sent a courier to reassure Sherman that he needed no assistance. However, Johnston's plan for a flank attack was upset by the late arrivals of Hardee, after the forced march that Private Ford was part of—the faulty maps had given Johnston the idea that Hardee was much closer to him than was in fact the case—and a need to reinforce Bragg, who was facing a Union assault on the Confederate left. Also in action were the Junior

A magazine engraving of Bentonville, the morning after the battle. *Courtesy of the North Carolina State Archives.*

Reserves, repulsing a Union brigade. After the battle, Walter Clark wrote to his mother that his command "attacked two Corps of Sherman's Army before the rest had come up and drove the Yanks two miles."[168]

Tired as Hardee's troops were, Johnston ordered them to attack at about three in the afternoon. They made a grand show for their few numbers—some regiments having no more than fifty men—and put two brigades to rout, but by this time Slocum understood what he was up against and had brought up more men, even his bummers. When Hardee paused to reorganize, he lost momentum and lost ground to a Federal assault. At this point Hoke, the North Carolinian released from Lee's command to help at Fort Fisher, joined combat for the first time that day, making what he considered an ill-advised frontal assault on orders from Braxton Bragg. Some of his men compared the ensuing firefight to the worst they had been through at Gettysburg and Cold Harbor. All in all, the day ended in a stalemate, with neither side having gained nor lost ground.[169]

By now alerted to what was happening on their left, units from Howard's command were being mobilized. They were "roused at 12 midnight with orders to draw one day's rations to do two days and prepare to march immediately," Jamison of the Tenth Illinois recalled. Hedley of the Thirty-second Illinois wrote of "a hard night's march over a miserable causeway built through the swamp. Rain fell in torrents all night long; the lightning was fearful, and one bolt struck a portion of the column, severely shocking several men." Union reinforcements arrived throughout the day on March 20—a day occupied with skirmishing and maneuvers more than pitched battle. Clark found the enemy attempting to swing around his post on the Confederate left end. "They were well repulsed," the young man wrote home.

> *I commanded the Skirmish line of our Brigade on Monday. It was in a good wood for skirmishing with little or no undergrowth. We had a regular Indian fight of it behind trees. They charged my line twice but were both times driven back. That night the whole skirmish line kept up an almost continuous firing as they expected our Army to leave. That together with the scamps trying to creep up on us in the dark kept us up all night.*[170]

For villagers in Bentonville itself, March 19–21 was "war and confusion and bold bloodshed," as witnessed by ten-year-old Dora Hood. Aware of what had happened to the west and south, townsfolk did their best to hide their silver, china, cash, horses and food. Dora's father, a prosperous carriage maker, hid his meat supply between the ceiling and the siding of the house, leaving her mother to worry that if the weather was warm, the grease would run and expose the precious provisions. The Hood yard became a hospital,

Right: Major Walter Clark, North Carolina Junior Reserves—the Confederacy's "seed corn." *From Angley et al.,* Clark's Papers.

Below: A cannon guards an open field at the Bentonville historic site.

making lifelong impressions on the child as men groaned while wounded arms and legs were amputated without benefit of anesthetic.

As if the Hoods did not have enough to worry about, Dora's father had been hauled off on suspicion of murdering a Union soldier and her brother was severely ill with measles. She was sent for help, and she made her way through a crowd of Union soldiers and horses, "pushing, running, crawling, anyway to reach, at last, the haven of the neighbor's house." There, however, Dora ran into Yankees busily ransacking the place and, as she was trying to get away, a soldier caught her and wanted to know where she thought she was going. Explaining her mission, Dora found herself up on the Yankee's horse and taken home, after which he went and fetched an army doctor. Despite the doctor's efforts, though, the brother died in the night.[171]

By Tuesday the twenty-first, Sherman had the bulk of his army on hand at Bentonville, and he launched a flanking move of his own to cut off Johnston's only line of retreat, which was through the village and over a lone bridge that spanned the swollen Mill Creek. The Confederate had begun sending his wounded to Smithfield on Monday night, and Tuesday was occupied in protecting his rear. Early that morning, Wheeler's men had built a line of breastworks, which an enemy charge turned at about 4:00 p.m. With the Federals all but in control of Johnston's only way out, Wheeler attacked, "feeling certain that the boldness and rapidity of a charge was all that could in any manner check a force so vastly our superior in numbers." His Texas Rangers "bore down most beautifully," charging through the enemy skirmishers and falling upon the Union line at the same moment as an Alabama squadron, "which threw the entire force of the enemy in a most

The Harper House served as a field hospital during the Bentonville battle.

rapid and disorderly retreat." Wheeler then established another defensive position and protected the creek while the rest of the army withdrew.[172]

While all this was going on, Schofield's army from the coast arrived at Cox's Bridge just west of Goldsboro, having met minimal resistance, and they began laying pontoons to assist Sherman's crossing. Among his troops were black units, honored veterans of the Fort Fisher assault. "Passing some of the finest plantations in the state," wrote J.A. Mowris, regimental surgeon of the 117th New York, "it was difficult to restrain the depredations of the negro troops as they witnessed again the comfort and opulence of their late task-masters."[173]

WEDNESDAY–THURSDAY, MARCH 22–23—GOLDSBORO AND SMITHFIELD

On Wednesday morning, Sherman sent Slocum's columns on to Goldsboro and ordered Howard to wait another day, not wanting to clog the roads. With the general, his aide Osborn went to have a look at the battleground,

> which has the characteristic of a battle field where a desperate battle has been fought. The graves of the enemy's dead, the dead horses, broken material, the lines of earth works, trees cut down with artillery, and the whole forest scarred and cut.

For the victory, Sherman gave all credit to Slocum and the stand he had made on the engagement's opening day. "It was his first great battle, and he fought it well," Osborn wrote in his journal—perhaps grudgingly, because Osborn admitted now that he had entertained a prejudice against the man. "His peculiarities are unpleasant," he noted.[174]

In retrospect, Sherman felt he had made a mistake in not attacking harder on the twenty-first, finishing Johnston then and there instead of letting him get away. The Wisconsin adjutant Edwin E. Bryant felt different:

A view of "Goldsborough." *Courtesy of the North Carolina State Archives.*

It is a blessing he so erred. What need of fighting any more battles, when the Confederacy was in the throes of its dying agony; what need that more precious lives be lost? Those splendid veterans, who had fought through the war, made that long march with such courage and fortitude, who had waded and corduroyed the Carolinas with such contempt for toil, danger, discomfort, should not be called to death or life-long maiming to fight a needless battle, just as the dawn-light of peace was ending the long, dark night of war.[175]

Bryant, of course, was writing with the benefit of a quarter-century's hindsight. On the other side of Mill Creek, the withdrawn Confederates were taking joy where they could find it in the immediate present. As Captain Bromfield Lewis Ridley wrote in his journal of March 23, "It is a treat that we are permitted to-day to wash up and put on clean clothes."[176]

General John Schofield joined forces with Sherman at Goldsboro. *Courtesy of the Bennett Place State Historic Site.*

Chapter Four

Wrapping Up

March 23–April 9 — Goldsboro and Smithfield

During the Bentonville fighting, more than five hundred Federal soldiers, and forty-five Confederates, were treated in the Harper family's home. For the historic site, the 1850s house has been furnished as a Civil War hospital, with an upstairs parlor and the dining room turned into surgeries, a downstairs parlor fitted out for minor operations and a bedroom for recuperating officers.

Afterward, the Union army transported its wounded to Goldsboro, while the Southerners were left in the Harper family's care. The Harpers buried those who died in their family cemetery. Years later those bodies, and others recovered from makeshift graves elsewhere on the battlefield, were disinterred and reburied in a mass grave a short distance east of the Harper House—beyond the visitors' center and its driveway, where a stone shaft atop a pyramidal base marks the spot beside a stand of pines. A single cannon guards the cemetery from behind the restored earthworks.

Wade Hampton was on hand for the dedication on the battle's thirtieth anniversary in 1895. By then, Hampton was an elder statesman, having been elected South Carolina's governor in 1876 and a United States senator in 1878. He served two terms in Washington, only to lose a reelection campaign to "Pitchfork" Ben Tillman in 1890 as the Populist movement swept into the South from the western Plains.

Wayne County Museum

After weeks of building toward a climactic meeting, Sherman and Johnston temporarily parted ways after Bentonville, leaving the present-day traveler with a decision: follow Sherman's advance to Goldsboro or Johnston's retreat to Smithfield. For the former, go east on Harper House Road to Cox

Railroad yards at Goldsboro were the goal of Sherman's march across the Carolinas.

Mill on the border of Johnston and Wayne counties; continue east and the road changes name to "Stevens Mill," and then to N.C. 581, before it brings you into Goldsboro and intersects with U.S. 70 Business. You should be on Ash Street. Turn right onto William Street, and stop into the Wayne County Museum, where a section describes "Goldsboro at War."

Exhibits have uniform jackets, bugles, swords and so forth. Also on display is a distinctive Union recruiting poster that reads, "Men of Color to Arms! To Arms! Now or never!" and a framed copy of the *New York Herald* of April 14, 1865, reporting:

> *Important*
> *Assassination of President Lincoln*
> *President shot at theater last evening*

And:

> *The Rebels*
> *Jeff Davis at Danville*
> *His latest appeal to his deluded followers*

But that's getting a little ahead of our story. Because Goldsboro is a military town, the museum has some more displays on other wars—the building, formerly home to the Goldsboro Woman's Club, served as civil defense headquarters and a USO club during World War II—and one particularly intriguing novelty, a gruesome looking permanent-wave machine from a beauty shop of the 1920s. There is also a diorama of the Battle of Goldsborough Bridge (the title retaining the "-ugh" spelling that was customary in the 1860s), a bloody affair of December 1862 when Union troops from New Berne attacked the Wilmington & Weldon railroad bridge south of town. The attack was briefly successful, but Confederates soon recaptured and rebuilt the bridge and held it until Schofield and Cox's arrival to meet Sherman more than two years later. The Goldsborough Bridge battlefield is open for self-guided touring, a short drive down U.S. 117.

Waynesborough Historical Village

While in Goldsboro, it is also worth some time to see the Waynesborough Historical Village, off U.S. 117 in the other direction. It is a collection of nineteenth-century buildings relocated to the site of Wayne County's original 1787 county seat, on a horseshoe bend in the Neuse River. The village of Waynesborough, named for Revolutionary War hero "Mad Anthony" Wayne, prospered for a while—until the railroad was laid a mile away in 1839. It was a terminal situation, and in 1845 some leading citizens proposed removing the county government to new and growing Goldsboro. That proposition failed, but upon reconsideration two years later voters changed their minds—helped along, the story goes, by relocation supporters who threw a barbecue during which a large quantity of white lightning was dumped into the closest well. By the time Sherman arrived, Waynesborough had dwindled to a few old buildings and docks, which Sherman burned. Eventually, Goldsboro bought the abandoned property for the city dump. Old Waynesborough came along with the Bicentennial inspired historic-preservation boom of the 1970s.[177]

While in Goldsboro, Sherman himself took over the home of a family named Washington, at 214 South Center Street—in a block now occupied by a fire station, illustrating, perhaps, that Goldsboro's municipal authorities do have a sense of humor. His troops remained in and around the town for two and a half weeks, resting and restoring themselves now that they were in communication with "the land of patriotism" and receiving supplies—like shoes—and mail from home.[178]

Their leader, having seen enough of his troops in review upon arrival, caught up his correspondence. To Grant, he described his distribution of

103

forces around Goldsboro, complained that the railroads in Union control were yet in disrepair, and advised, "If I get the troops all well placed, and the supplies working well, I might run up to see you." He wrote to his wife, Ellen, in Chicago, catching her up on what had happened since Fayetteville, reported the army was "dirty ragged & Saucy," offered some advice about handling the children and gently chided her about taking part in a charity bazaar: "I don't much approve of ladies selling things at a table."[179]

Sherman, and his troops, could well feel satisfied. "We had in mid-winter accomplished the whole journey of four hundred and twenty-five miles in fifty days," the general wrote in his *Memoirs*, "averaging ten miles per day, allowing ten lay-days, and had reached Goldsboro' with the army in superb order."[180] Major Henry Hitchcock realized there had been a close call at Bentonville:

> *Undoubtedly if, (yes, if) J.J.'s attack on Slocum on Sunday had succeeded in "mashing up" that part of our force, it would have been a severe blow.* [But as it turned out] *Johnston's hopes of dividing and beating us are a dead failure.*[181]

Osborn, the artillery colonel from New York, was not so sanguine.

> *Our work is not done yet. General Lee's army is at Richmond and General Johnston's army is in front of us. A few other detachments are in the south and west…The next campaign will bring the armies of Generals Lee and Johnston together between here and Richmond where a general battle would be fought.*[182]

Sherman and Grant, also, figured there was one more big battle ahead. Their own commander was hoping this was not the case. Two days after reaching Goldsboro, Sherman left for the "run up" to see Grant—taking a locomotive to Morehead City on the coast, then a steamer up into the Chesapeake Bay and the James River to City Point, Virginia, with a brief stop-off to wire his brother, United States Senator John Sherman, an invitation to ride back to North Carolina with him. On Tuesday March 28, Sherman and Grant held a council of war with President Lincoln, advising him that they expected "one or the other of us would have to fight one more bloody battle." The president said, several times, there had been enough bloodshed already.

"All he wanted of us was to defeat the opposing armies, and to get the men composing the Confederate armies back to their homes, at work on their farms and in their shops," Sherman recalled. Lincoln even hoped that

Jefferson Davis would find some way to slip out of the country and go away, without capture, and spare the need for a trial.

> *I know, when I left him,, that I was more than ever impressed by his kindly nature, his deep and earnest sympathy with the afflictions of the whole people…and by the march of hostile armies through the South; and that his earnest desire seemed to be to end the war speedily, without more bloodshed or devastation, and to restore all the men of both sections to their homes…I never saw him again.*[183]

While the Union command felt assured final victory was near, some Confederates were feeling optimistic as well. At Smithfield, Johnston received reinforcements as troops from Georgia finally reached his camps, along with men scattered from their units at Bentonville, and he was in a good position to observe his adversary.

> *It was uncertain whether his march to Virginia would be through Raleigh, or by the most direct route, that through Weldon. So the Confederate army was placed between the two roads, in order to be able to precede him on either; and, to make the junction of the Army of Northern Virginia with it practicable, should General Lee determine to abandon his intrenchments [sic] to fall upon Sherman's army with our united forces.*[184]

Confederates shared other sentiments with their Yankee counterparts. Captain Ridley recorded:

> *Soldiering in these piney woods is more disagreeable than any I have yet experienced. The smoke tans your skin, soils your clothes, and one presents a spectacle like that of an engineer who has worked sometime on his engine without change…*
>
> *We saw a squad of forty Yanks [prisoners]…From their brazen looks, they consider us virtually whipped, and that our complete overthrow is only a question of time. Numbers may subdue but cannot conquer.*[185]

And young Clark, writing to his mother on March 27 after receiving a package from home:

> *My shirts suited me exactly. They are very pretty and have been much admired. My Box came just in the nick of time and was I think the best you ever sent me. At least it seemed so while it lasted. I can't imagine where you got so many eggs. Not one of them was broken.*[186]

Bentonville

To catch up with Johnston now, retrace the route from Goldsboro to Bentonville and from Harper House Road turn north onto Devil's Racetrack Road, Route 1009. Shortly you come to Bentonville itself, a small village that the Union surgeon J.A. Mowris described:

> *Scarcely a dozen small unpainted weather-beaten dwellings. Two or three of these primitive tenements, were still occupied by several severely wounded rebel soldiers. They were destitute of hospital conveniences, were indifferently attended and appeared to be subsisting on the plainest quality of food. Besides the wounded soldiers, the population of the Village, consisted of three or four very poor families.* [187]

Now there is little more than some abandoned buildings and a brick Community Building. Crossing two creeks and continuing north, you come to a Civil War Trails kiosk at the intersection of Stewart Road. Devil's Racetrack follows the route Johnston took to Bentonville, and on March 22, Hardee wrote to him from "this wretched road, which I have been working on and pulling wagons through all the morning."

Johnston had other fronts to deal with, too. A courier arrived from General Samuel Jones in Tallahassee, Florida:

> *We are so greatly in need of funds to pay the troops in this district and to meet the ordinary current expenses of the service, and mail communication with you and with Richmond so very precarious and uncertain, that I send a quartermaster, Major Hamilton, directly to your headquarters for funds. Besides many other outstanding debts, the troops have not been paid since last August. Some of them never have been paid.* [188]

Beauregard, now in Raleigh, sent repeated dispatches asking what to do with supplies in that city and with railroad rolling stock. Hampton speculated that Union General Phil Sheridan might be on the way with six thousand cavalrymen from the Shenandoah Valley. Governor Vance and the newspapers were receiving repeated complaints about the behavior of Wheeler's foragers in the countryside, to the point that several of Wheeler's subordinate officers made a public testimonial on the general's behalf. And Johnston was busy defending his own reputation in the face of accusations in John Bell Hood's much-publicized report on Atlanta's loss. In an exchange of angry telegrams, Johnston informed Hood that he meant to call him to account before a court-martial. [189]

In camp, Walter Clark was fed up with what went on up the chain of command, military and otherwise.

> *If the Federals had the appointing of men & direction of affairs they could not have done more for our injury than we have ourselves…When we begin to strip the speculators, beat drunken officers & place both in the ranks I then shall have a shadow of a hope.*[190]

The news from elsewhere was discouraging, too. On March 30, Clark's father, David, wrote him from the family home on the Roanoke River:

> *Some of the Home Guard officers seem to think that organization a force & have come to my conclusion that the Militia alone should be organized & put on a war footing as Minute Men (Mounted). I think it would be well…They should protect the farmers from the depredations of stragglers for the amount of these rascals is causing immense damage to the cause. Men are actually afraid to leave home as they do not know at what time the plunderers might come & strip their families of everything, leaving them without anything to eat & nothing to look forward to as they take every horse & mule—People cannot send supplies for they cannot know into what hands the wagons & teams might fall even in a few miles of Home…Your cousin Ed Nicholson was killed last Saturday at Petersburg.*[191]

The route of Johnston's retreat soon became that of Yankee advance. On April 10, Sherman began the march that would prove to be his army's last of the war, and by that time events elsewhere had totally changed the situation. On March 25, Lee's troops made an offensive move from their trenches, capturing some ground but quickly losing it and prompting Grant to counterattack around Lee's southernmost flank. On April 1, Sheridan overwhelmed Confederate defenders at Five Forks, southwest of Petersburg, and the next morning a massive assault drove Lee out of his fortifications and into retreat along the Appomattox River. Jefferson Davis got the news during church on the morning of April 2, and left worship to organize his government's own retreat from Richmond. Word reached Johnston's camp three days later.

> *We, to-day, have heard of the distressing news that the fall of Richmond took place…Heavens, the gloom and how terrible our feelings! A city that had been protected for four years now to succumb to the world's minions— Lee has to give up and leave the bones of our braves behind…*
>
> *It never rains but it pours, and still the bad news comes—Selma, Alabama, we hear officially, has been given up to a raiding party. 'Tis*

said, too, that a column of nine thousand Yanks have entered it. We heard to-day from Richmond that Lee lost all his artillery but two battalions, supposed to have been about 500 pieces. Of his loss in men we have not yet heard. General S. takes the death of his little boy at Auburn, Ala., very hard.[192]

On April 6, the governor and some ladies came down from Raleigh to review and cheer the decimated force at Smithfield. And news came of a proclamation, calling on the Southern people to stand firm, from Jefferson Davis, who was by then at Danville, almost at the North Carolina line.

APRIL 3–10—RALEIGH, DANVILLE

Devil's Racetrack Road will connect with U.S. 301—the old Florida highway—at the edge of Smithfield, and will take you past another Trails kiosk at the Highway Patrol station by Moccasin Creek. According to the text there, after meeting Rebel skirmishers en route, Sherman's troops burned several homes and shops, and the general commented, "Poor North Carolina will have a hard time, for we sweep the country like a swarm of locusts." Johnston pulled back to Raleigh before Sherman's advance, leaving Smithfield for the Union's occupation on April 11.

Wyatt's Memorial

From Smithfield, the most direct way to Raleigh is by U.S. 70, but it is a slow and aggravating ride, stoplight to stoplight, through the widespread suburbs of the Raleigh-Durham Triangle. A more pleasant way is to turn from 301 onto U.S. 70 Business through town, perhaps stopping to visit the Ava Gardner Museum on the main drag, Market Street (Smithfield is the movie star's hometown), and the Johnston County Heritage Center one block farther on. Crossing the Neuse River and leaving town, bear off left onto N.C. 210 and take a twenty-minute drive in the country before reaching Interstate 40. Take it to the Raleigh Beltline (I-440), and exit onto Saunders Street going north into the city and Capitol Square. The 1840 Greek Revival capitol is on the National Register of Historic Places, and on its shady grounds there are two memorials to the "Recent Unpleasantness."

On the west side, a sentry stands atop a tall spire, flanked by a pair of naval cannon the Confederates took from the Norfolk, Virginia harbor in 1861. Nearby, Private Henry Lawson Wyatt has charged the enemy in immortal bronze since June 10, 1912, when the North Carolina Division of

A Confederate memorial at the Old State Capitol, Raleigh—it faces west out Hillsborough Street, the Rebels' line of retreat.

the United Daughters of the Confederacy erected his likeness, honoring the first Confederate to fall in combat.

A carpenter in Edgecombe County, in North Carolina's northeastern quadrant, Wyatt was actually a Virginian by birth but moved to North Carolina at age fourteen. Called to the colors in April 1861, he signed up with the Edgecombe Guards, first of the state's units to take the field, for a six-month hitch. On June 10, 1861, Wyatt's unit engaged the Yankees at Big Bethel, near Hampton, Virginia. He and several other men were ordered to attack and burn a house that was providing the enemy with cover. Wyatt went down with a musket ball in his head, thus providing one-third of the inspiration for a North Carolina motto: "First at Bethel, farthest at Gettysburg, last at Appomattox."

Wyatt's memorial also bears the names of five comrades who made the charge with him: George T. Williams, John H. Thorpe, Robert H. Ricks, Robert H. Bradley and Thomas Fallon. Curiously enough, his statue is placed with Wyatt facing north—opposite the direction from which Sherman's Yankees entered Raleigh in 1865, such that his attacking pose suggests rather eternal retreat. Similarly, the generic monument faces west, out Hillsborough Street, the route of Confederate withdrawal rather than Federal invasion—a south-facing statue of George Washington is symbolically left to handle the Yankees by himself.

Oakwood Cemetery

Not far from the old statehouse there are two other sites deserving a pause to pay respects. From Capitol Square, go east on Morgan Street and turn left onto Person. Go four blocks, then turn right onto Oakwood and, at the foot of a hill, turn left into Oakwood Cemetery. The Confederate Cemetery will be on your right, spread over a hillside beyond a stone archway and above a Hall of Memory, an open arcade whose walls bear commemorative plaques.

Marked by a Confederate first national flag—the Stars and Bars, rather than the more common Southern Cross battle flag—1,388 Confederate soldiers, 1,092 from North Carolina, lie there in ranks beneath gleaming white headstones. Along with one Yankee. In 2007, a grave long thought to hold an unknown Southern solider was found to in fact hold the remains

Henry Wyatt memorial in Capitol Square, Raleigh. Wyatt was the first Confederate soldier to fall in action in Big Bethel, Virginia, June 1861.

A Confederate plot in Oakwood Cemetery, Raleigh.

of Private John O. Dolson, a Minnesotan who fell at Gettysburg. Upon that discovery, Dolson received a proper identification on his marker and a proper military remembrance service by a local Union reenactor unit.

In a way, Dolson's presence is appropriate. During the war, soldiers from both sides were treated in Raleigh hospitals, and those who died there or in fighting close by were interred in a common burying ground. Within a year after the war's end, the ladies of Raleigh found the graves in a state of neglect and formed a memorial association to honor the resting places of fallen Confederates.

In 1866, though, Raleigh was an occupied city. Late that year, a Reconstruction official decided the cemetery should be reserved for the winning side and Union dead from battleground graves at Bentonville should be relocated. Raleigh Mayor W.H. Harrison was ordered to get the Rebs out of the ground before they were tossed into the street. So, on February 22, 1867—George Washington's birthday—citizens turned out to move the remains of 538 Southern boys to a site donated for the purpose by resident Henry Mordecai, though occupation authorities forbade procession, prayers, consecration or any other act of remembrance, on pain of being shot.

Private John O. Dolson's grave at Oakwood was identified and marked in 2007. Dolson, a Minnesotan who fell at Gettysburg, was buried as a Confederate by mistake.

Still defiant, Raleigh's un-Reconstructed womenfolk left flowers and personal items and set a memorial observance on May 10—the fourth anniversary of Stonewall Jackson's death. The day was rainy and the Yankee soldiers were on guard, but citizens still gathered at the capitol and marched to decorate the graves. As if not to be outdone, a year later the occupation troops processed from the capitol to what is now Raleigh National Cemetery, led by a black army band and accompanied by a crowd of freedmen to decorate graves of the Federal dead.

To visit the Union graves, leave Oakwood and continue east on Oakwood Avenue to Tarboro Road and turn right. Tarboro will become Rock Quarry Road, and the cemetery will be on your left, enclosed by a low brick wall. The Gettysburg Address is posted at the entrance, and Civil War casualties are concentrated in the northwest corner:

> *James B. Hawkins, 1ˢᵗ Sgt. Co. H 50ᵗʰ Regiment Illinois Infantry*
> *Jay Allen US Soldier March 30 1865*
> *Frederick Uts, Co F 82ⁿᵈ Regiment Illinois Infantry March 27, 1865*
> *Unknown US Soldier.*

Caswell County

Leaving Sherman behind for the time being on the Raleigh road, this is a good point for an advance of the traveler's own. With Robert E. Lee in retreat and Jefferson Davis in flight, the next developments for the war in North Carolina would take place to the west. To follow their course, consider an excursion to meet the Confederate president at the Confederacy's last capital, just over the state line.

From the National Cemetery, go south on Rock Quarry Road to the Inner Beltline (I-440 clockwise) and exit onto I-40 going west toward Durham. Past the Raleigh-Durham airport, bear right onto N.C. 147, the Durham Freeway, and go through Durham to I-85. Exit onto U.S. 70 toward Hillsborough, take the Bypass route and turn right onto N.C. 86 for another free-breathing ride through rolling open country. It takes about forty-five minutes.

Relatively peaceful during the war, this area turned violent afterwards with vigilantism and reprisals by the old guard Ku Klux Klan and the Union League of freedmen and their white allies. Among the latter was

"Last Confederate Capitol"—Sutherlin House, now the Danville Museum of Fine Arts and History.

John Walter Stephens, a civilian agent for the Confederate army during the war who afterwards became a Republican and worked for the Freedmen's Bureau and Union League in Caswell County on the Virginia border. Caswell had been a prosperous agricultural county in the early 1800s, its location on the Dan River and near Virginia's roads giving it access to outside markets—unlike most of North Carolina's capital-bleeding interior prior to railroad construction. It was in Caswell, in 1839, that a slave blacksmith named Stephen on the Abisha Slade plantation accidentally discovered a method for curing brightleaf tobacco that, in decades to come, would be the foundation for North Carolina's cigarette industry.

With its prosperity, Caswell County enjoyed considerable power in antebellum state politics, a base disrupted by the war and Reconstruction. When black support raised "Chicken" Stephens (so nicknamed for the object of a dispute with a neighbor) to the state senate in 1868, he became a pariah to white residents, accused but never convicted of burning farms and even killing his own mother. In 1870, the animosity climaxed in Stephens's murder on the courthouse steps in Yanceyville, which set off a veritable civil war in that section of the state. The 1861 courthouse still stands downtown along with more than twenty other pre–Civil War buildings, including an 1810 residence housing the county's historical museum.[193] Your road passes through the edge of Yanceyville (population about twenty-six hundred).

The Confederacy's Last Capitol

Approaching Virginia, you pass a historical marker indicating that George Washington slept nearby—during his Southern tour of 1791. Crossing the state line, come into Danville and bear off to the right onto South Main Street and look for a park-like block on the right at the top of a hill. This is the grounds of the Sutherlin House, now the Danville Museum of Fine Arts and History, but for a week in 1865 it served as the Confederacy's last capitol.

"Between the Lines: Danville 1861–1865, drifting toward disaster" is a permanent exhibit here, where you find a copy of Virginia's "Ordinance to Repeal the Ratification of the Constitution of the United States of America By the State of Virginia to Resume All Rights and Powers Granted Under Said Constitution." There are weapons and military gear on display, along with 1860s surgical instruments, for Danville was a hospital town as well as a prisoner of war facility. Union captives are represented by a uniformed mannequin that sits in a six- by six-foot cell. Prisoners were accommodated in tobacco warehouses, and more than thirteen hundred Federal soldiers' remains lie in a nearby cemetery. Most died of smallpox.

Confederate President Jefferson
Davis, in his younger days. *Courtesy
of the Danville Museum.*

A Union prisoner—or his
mannequin stand-in—in "Between
the Lines: Danville 1861–1865"
permanent exhibition at the
Danville Museum.

The Rebel government picked Danville for a refuge because the town's location and existing fortifications made it a likely point for Lee's army to regroup. Davis and his entourage arrived after a twenty-four-hour train ride from Richmond, a ride that one of the president's companions describes in an exhibit:

> *The track was dangerously bad and the locomotives wheezing, steaming and burning nearly twice their normal amount of wood would make barely 12 miles per hour. Sometimes the track would spread apart and we would stop and spike it down and go ahead. At other times, the old engine would stop from sheer exhaustion. Then we would get out and walk up the grade, then get aboard and away again.*

On April 4, Davis issued his "Last Proclamation" from Danville.

> *The memories of the heroic dead who have freely given their lives in* [the Confederacy's] *defense must ever remain enshrined in our hearts. Let us not, then, despond, my countrymen; but, relying on the never-failing mercies*

The locomotive that, with great difficulty, brought Davis and his government to Danville just before Richmond fell. *Courtesy of the Danville Museum.*

"THE LAST PROCLAMATION"
... THE MEMORIES OF THE HEROIC
DEAD WHO HAVE FREELY GIVEN THEIR
LIVES TO ITS DEFENSE MUST EVER
REMAIN ENSHRINED IN OUR HEARTS...
PRESIDENT JEFFERSON DAVIS
C. S. A.
APRIL 4, 1865

Above: The "Last Proclamation" memorial on the Danville Museum lawn.

Right: The Union *Sixth Corps* newspaper, printed in Danville after occupation. *Courtesy of the Danville Museum.*

and protecting care of our God, let us meet the foe with fresh defiance, with unconquered and unconquerable hearts.

On April 10, Captain W.P. Graves arrived with official notice that Lee had surrendered to Grant at Appomattox Court House the day before—Palm Sunday. Davis and his ministers pulled up stakes and fled farther south, to Greensboro, safely behind Johnston's lines, leaving Danville to be occupied by the enemy. A Union corps soon arrived—the same unit that broke the Rebel lines at Petersburg—and, among other acts, it leased the *Danville Register* newspaper and hired its editor to supervise publication of a paper of its own. The April 27, 1865 edition is on display, with a column bylined "Owenisko":

> *I know of no opposition except the river which, by the way, was running rapidly…The citizens were delighted to see us and many were seen to cross themselves before our glorious banner…The business prospects of Danville are decidedly promising. Major—is informed the ladies of Danville are already disposed in favor of Union soldiers.*

TUESDAY–THURSDAY, APRIL 11–13—GREENSBORO, RALEIGH

From Danville, it is an hour's drive down U.S. 29 to Greensboro, where the city's history museum displays a large collection of Confederate firearms. Take the Summit Avenue exit, go into downtown and turn left at Church Street. The museum there occupies the site of a Civil War hospital, for Greensboro, too, was receiving casualties by the hundreds—two hundred sick and wounded on the courthouse floor alone.[194] Johnston, in Raleigh, got word of Lee's surrender at 1:00 a.m. on the eleventh. Later that morning, the last of his troops pulled out of Smithfield, burning the Neuse River Bridge behind them, and marched west to the state's capital.

> *Started about 7 o'clock this morning and pitched tents three miles west of Raleigh on the Hillsboro road. Have heard nothing of enemy's progress. As we passed the female seminary in Raleigh the beautiful school girls greeted us warmly. Each one had a pitcher of water and goblet. We drank, took their addresses, and had a big time. It was a terrible task to get Terry, Cahil, Caruthers, Stewart, and the other members of the staff away from them. On this march my faithful boy, Hannibal, gladdened us with a rich box of edibles from my old grandmother at Oxford.[195]*

Johnston received a summons from Davis late in the afternoon and boarded a train for Greensboro, arriving about eight in the morning of April 12. Davis received him with a "pep talk"—insisting that the cause only needed its deserters to return to arms. Johnston replied that men who had left before the army was in such dire straits would hardly be inclined to rejoin it now. Davis dismissed any such notion, and his general, and told Johnston to wait around until the acting Secretary of War John C. Breckinridge could join them later on.[196]

The Confederate president was one of few Southerners then holding such an opinion, but he was not alone. On the tenth, William Clark had written his mother from Smithfield:

> *Our Army I am glad to say is continually increasing. I do not think affairs can remain in this state of suspense much longer. Something decisive must be done shortly. It is beyond my ken to see any end to the War but while I am able for service I intend to stand by the cause while a banner floats to tell where Freedom and freedom's sons still support her cause…*

Joseph Eggleston Johnston, in later life. *From Johnson,* Memoir.

In the numerous desertions from our Army and the consequent fall of Richmond & Petersburg we but behold the result of the senseless despondency of our people in [18]64. If the people are deserving of Freedom; if they are fit to be a Nation the struggle can not close but with the complete success to our Arms.

But he added a sober note:

Johnston's Army has on its Muster Rolls nearly 175,000 men fit for service. Of this 45,000 are present. Quite a contrast. Lee's Army I suppose is much the same way.

Clark was right that the "state of suspense" was near its end, and about the manpower available, but he, like his president, had lost touch with reality. Grant was victorious, and Sherman's army was well rested and ready to put an end to business. Shortly before leaving Goldsboro, Hitchcock had written:

Indeed it is wonderful how quickly and how completely the pitching of a few tents and the busy movement of their inhabitants, the bright crackling of camp-fires and the sound of human voices—sometimes merry, sometimes mad, depending much upon the weather,—will metamorphose a muddy hill-top or a lonely bit of pine-woods, into a scene full of interest and imagination.[197]

Lieutenant Colonel Nichols, the once and future journalist on Sherman's staff, found the country pleasing as he came up to Smithfield, "rich in corn and fodder" with handsome homes and wheat fields that reminded the men of Ohio and Wisconsin. "The people," he wrote, "are intelligent, and profess a sort of half-way Unionism—*i.e.*, they want the war closed." He was taken aback, though, by the sight of public stocks on the Smithfield town square: "that relic of the past…Our progressive soldiers cut down the machine and burned it." However, his spirits were brightened by the Neuse Riverbanks "lined with beautiful flowering shrubs, and clothed with the fresh green of spring"; and by newspaper reports from Alabama, Tennessee and western North Carolina that Federal forces were advancing on all fronts.[198]

While Johnston was meeting with Davis, word was spreading through Sherman's ranks that Lee had given up the fight. At one point:

Tremendous cheering—men's guns go down and their hats go up! Army wild with joy. Brigade massed and dispatch read. Cheers for Grant, for Sherman and for 3d Brigade![199]

At another:

> On the 12th, while on the march, a staff officer galloped back, spreading the news that Lee had surrendered. "You are the man we've been looking for, for four years," cried the joyous soldiers. They cheered and cheered. Then they yelled and hugged one another; and the word went through the lines, "We must push Jo. Johnston now."[200]

At a third:

> The procession was halted and the message announced, when a shout went up from thousands of throats; such an acclamation as those "valleys and rocks never heard." And away it rolled back down the winding column, and again it swelled forth, while the air overhead was literally filled with hats, haversacks and belts, and even guns and swords were seen making summersaults at an unusual height. Here and there too might be seen warm handshakings and cordial gratulations at the news, and those who have experienced the privations and perils of soldier life, will not be surprised to learn that there were even tears of joy…Here at last was victory, for the sacrifice, and a joy for past humiliation.[201]

While the Northern boys were marching "with light step and eager hearts," as Nichols put it, North Carolina authorities were taking matters into their own hands. Vance sent former governors William Graham and David Swain on a peace mission to Sherman. Along the way, the emissaries were intercepted and detained twice—first by Wade Hampton, who had a message from Hardee revoking their passage through Confederate lines; then, with Hampton's men under attack by Kilpatrick's cavalry, their train advanced another mile or so before meeting a Union squad that took the dignitaries into custody after relieving them of their valuables. After putting up with several hours' rude treatment and mockery, some from Kilpatrick himself, Graham, Swain and their companions were escorted to see Sherman and enjoyed a more hospitable reception. Sherman assured them of safe passage back to Raleigh and assured the state government of his protection and desire to work with it to terminate hostilities. Vance, in the meantime, directed Raleigh Mayor Harrison to surrender the city when the time came.[202]

Eighty miles west, Breckinridge arrived, and on the morning of April 13, Johnston and Beauregard, who had met him in Greensboro, went for another meeting with Davis. Now, at the president's invitation, Johnston delivered his opinion that the country was tired of war, overrun, with resources near exhaustion and soldiers walking away from the fight.

Beauregard added his full agreement. Davis asked what he should do, and Johnston suggested he contact Sherman, general to general, and see what terms could be arranged. Davis agreed, a message was written and sent ahead for Hampton, who was headquartered at Hillsborough, instructing him to handle delivery.[203]

The Confederate army abandoned Raleigh, and Sherman arrived on Thursday the thirteenth, in a heavy rain that did nothing to dampen his soldiers' spirits.

> *Marching up the main street to the tune of "Hail Columbia," a halt was made at the capitol and our arms stacked on the square. As details for protection were called for by the citizens, guards were sent with them, so that in a short time the One Hundred and Fourth [Illinois] was scattered all over town. Raleigh was the prettiest looking city we had seen in the South, the houses were mostly large and in good condition, the gardens full of flowers and the air fragrant everywhere.*[204]

The North Carolina capital made good impressions generally on the occupation troops, with its trees, "elegant private residences" and stately capitol building—though the latter's interior was found in a state of mess when Mowris, the surgeon, looked in:

> *Bound legislative documents, and maps, lay strewn about the floor of the library. The museum rooms were in even a worse plight. The sash and glass of the cases had been broken, and many of the specimens of natural history had been "confiscated." The geological collections had been wantonly broken and promiscuously scattered…On a shelf behind the speaker's desk, was a marble bust, on the base of which in relief were the words "John C. Calhoun." Poised on its crown, was an inverted inkstand, whose contents had descended in copious streams over the face. The marks of a brush or cloth charged with the same fluid, had still more besmutted the features. Under the name, in pencil, was written this explanatory clause. "Yes, father of Secessionism."*[205]

Nichols, however, blamed the Confederates under Wheeler for what "pillage and outrage" Raleigh suffered.

> *They seem to make no distinction between friend and foe where plunder is possible. All through Georgia and South Carolina and now in the capital of the old North State, the same scenes of lawlessness have been witnessed. They broke open the stores and entered the houses, robbing their own people of every*

thing they could get their hands upon, adding to theft such acts of personal violence as would have been shameful cowardice, if visited upon an enemy.[206]

While some Union troops were restoring order in the city, Wheeler's horsemen were fighting a running skirmish with Kilpatrick's men along the railroad running west. At three in the afternoon, Kilpatrick reported from Morrisville Station:

I have pressed the rebels back two miles beyond this town on road to Chapel Hill. His cavalry is totally demoralized. We have taken barricade after barricade of the strongest character and with but little loss. Prisoners and citizens report the rebel transportation in very bad condition. I have been scattering Wheeler's cavalry all day, driving it off upon the side roads. I have captured three trains, without the engines, of about seven cars each, loaded with stores of different kinds taken from the wagon trains, which they had evidently come down to relieve. We dashed on an engine and a portion of my people was within 100 yards of it, but the enemy was too strong for them and it escaped. I have captured a large quantity of corn, shelled, on the cars at this point, fully sufficient for my command. The cars are in good condition, roads are bad. I have marched a long ways to-day and fought over nearly every foot of ground from Raleigh to this point. I shall rest my command and allow it to close up.[207]

FRIDAY–SUNDAY, APRIL 14–16—HILLSBOROUGH, DURHAM'S STATION

Today, Hillsborough is a forty-five-minute trip from Greensboro by way of Interstate 85. Johnston's trip by train took somewhat longer, but he arrived on the morning of April 14, informed his army of Lee's surrender and waited to hear back from Sherman.

Dickson House

While much of Johnston's force was still retreating west, Hampton had settled in at the eighteenth-century home of Alexander Dickson, south of the colonial town that had been a hotbed of Regulator activity during the backcountry rising of 1771, a seat for the state legislature during the Revolution and home to William Hooper, a signer of the Declaration of Independence. By the mid-1800s it was an affluent place with about one thousand residents, the military academy and a girls' school and a number

The "office," used by Johnston and Hampton, at the Dickson House in Hillsborough.

of influential citizens. By mid-April 1865 it was crowded with refugees from Sherman's march and the prevailing disorder. In its April 5 edition, the *Recorder* had reported "heavy fighting" near Petersburg, accounts of Yankee depredations at Fayetteville, the news of Sherman's and Schofield's arrival at Goldsboro and a notice of locations where the county assessors would be listing taxes.[208] It was the newspaper's last issue for some weeks to come.

The original Dickson homesite is now occupied by a shopping center, but the house itself stands on King Street in downtown Hillsborough where it serves as a visitor center. Take the Churton Street exit from the interstate, go left through the gas station and fast-food strip, up a hill and down past the historic markers and turn right onto King Street. The house is on the right at the end of the street. The outbuilding that Johnston and Hampton used is in the side yard beside a garden, furnished as a nineteenth-century farm office with desk, paper from the Southern Telegraph Companies and a book of sample business letters; also part of a spinning wheel, hanging herbs, pots and kettle on the hearth and a pair of sheep shears.

Morrisville

From Hillsborough, rejoin the Union lines at Morrisville, where Kilpatrick had spent the night of April 13. Take I-85 to the Durham Freeway, merge into I-40 and turn off at the second Morrisville exit onto Aviation Parkway. Cross N.C. 54 and the railroad—you're at a spot where Kilpatrick and Wheeler skirmished with rifles and artillery as residents hid in their basements and an overloaded train, carrying Confederate wounded and supplies, struggled to get up enough steam to move. Eventually, a sensible trainman uncoupled the freight cars and the train made its getaway—a story long lost until local historian Ernie Dollar scoured out the details from musty letters, diaries and dispatches, and, since April 2000, commemorated by a historic marker at the Town Hall. It was also at Morrisville that, around midnight, Confederate Captain Rawlins Lowndes arrived under a flag of truce with Johnston's letter to Sherman.

Kilpatrick invited Lowndes to stay the night and wait for Sherman's reply. The Rebel and his hosts passed some time trading barbs over battles past, concluding when Lowndes challenged Kilpatrick to meet Hampton with fifteen hundred Yankees against one thousand Southerners, and fight it out with sabers. At that point, everyone went to bed.[209]

Sherman got the message on the morning of the fourteenth and immediately replied.

> *I am fully empowered to arrange with you any terms for the suspension of further hostilities between the armies commanded by you and those commanded by myself, and will be willing to confer with you to that end…I really desire to save the people of North Carolina the damage they would sustain by the march of this army.*[210]

Kilpatrick, meanwhile, split his own command, sending one wing west toward the university town of Chapel Hill and going himself with the other wing north along the railroad to Durham's Station—a fuel and water stop with about a hundred residents. Sherman had directed that his reply to Johnston be sent on as quickly as possible, but Kilpatrick, by some accounts distrusting the Confederates' intentions, dawdled with the result that it was not until late on Saturday, the fifteenth, that the message reached Hampton and Johnston. Johnston immediately took a train to Greensboro, only to find that Davis was already gone, having fled to Charlotte. Hampton made arrangements for the generals' meeting on Monday, on the road between Hillsborough and Durham's Station—that is, in the no man's land between the Union and Confederate forward lines. While the commanders were exchanging letters, their cavalries continued their skirmishing, fighting their last on the rainy night of April 15 along New Hope Creek, near present-day Stagecoach Road in southern Durham County.[211] In North Carolina, no one yet knew that Abraham Lincoln was dead.

Sunday–Tuesday, April 16–17—Durham

While the Union army relaxed in Raleigh and the Confederates were trudging west, foragers and scavengers from both sides were roaming the country between Raleigh and Hillsborough, calling upon small farms as well as the area's few real plantations. Just west of New Hope Creek, the land rises into a sandy ridge that in the antebellum period had proved good for cotton culture. Richard Stanford Leigh, third generation of his family in what was then still eastern Orange County, had settled on five hundred acres there in 1835 and by the Civil War's outbreak had amassed almost one thousand acres that he worked with his family and fourteen slaves. Yankee bummers paid him a call, liberating his smokehouse, corncrib and whatever else they could find, but, according to family lore, he was eventually reimbursed for the loss and used the cash to put up a new gristmill. Leigh needed all the production he could get from his lands—he was father to twenty children.[212]

Union officers hamming for a portrait photographer, location unknown. *Courtesy of the North Carolina State Archives.*

Slave cabin at Leigh Farm in Durham County.

Since the mid-1990s, Leigh Farm has been a public park "under development" by the city of Durham. Development is minimal, but it is open for a visitor to see the farmhouse, carriage house (with a curious extension added to give room for motorcars), dairy and a slave cabin with a chimney built of sticks—unusual, for reasons that should be obvious. To reach the park from Morrisville, take I-40 toward Chapel Hill and take Exit 273 onto N.C. 54, going east; very quickly, turn left onto Leigh Farm Road and follow it as it narrows to a single lane through woods to the homestead.

Historic Stagville

For a plantation on another scale, take I-40 west again, exiting onto U.S. 15–501 toward Durham and follow its bypass to I-85 north. Go toward Richmond, and exit at Red Mill Road. You're out in the country again now; turn left at the foot of the exit ramp and drive a ways, passing Chewning Middle School, until the road ends at a *T* intersection. Turn right, left, then right onto the Old Oxford Highway—look for the Scenic Byway sign—and go on to Historic Stagville, a state historic site that preserves a small portion of what was North Carolina's largest plantation complex.

Established in the eighteenth century by merchant Richard Bennehan, the operation boomed as it passed down the family to Bennehan's son-in-law, Duncan Cameron of Hillsborough, and his son, Paul. By 1865, the

Richard Stanford Leigh received partial compensation for a Union raid on his farm on New Hope Creek.

Bennehan-Cameron holdings covered thirty thousand acres and employed almost one thousand slaves in North Carolina alone, with more lands and slaves in Alabama and Mississippi. The present-day site includes a well-preserved slave quarter from 1850, a monumental barn built by slave craftsmen in 1860—testimony to the assurance its owners felt even at the verge of their society's collapse—and the original big house, begun in 1787, and a surprise for any visitor who comes expecting Tara. By the war, the family had built a more stylish home nearby, Fairntosh, which is still privately owned and occupied. One of the former Cameron slaves, Cy Hart, told an interviewer in the 1930s what happened when the bummers came. His story was set down in dialect:

> *One day some of Wheeler's men came and dey tried to take what dey wanted, but Marse Paul* [Cameron] *had de silver money an' other things hid. Dey wanted us niggers to tell dem where everythin' wus, but we said we didn' know nuthin'. Marse Paul was hid in de woods wid de horses an' some of de other stock…*
>
> *Den Wheeler's men saw de Yankees comin' and dey run away. De Yankees chased dem to de bridge an' dey done some fightin' an' one or two of Wheeler's men wus killed an' de rest got away.*

The Horton Grove slave village at Stagville plantation in Durham County.

Den de captain of de Yankees come to Mammy's cabin an' axed her whar de meat house an' flour an sech at. She tole him dat Pappy had de keys to go an' ax him. "Ax him nothin'," de captain said. He called some of his men and dey broke down de door to de meat house. Den dey trowed out plenty of dose hams an' dey tole Mammy to cook dem somethin' to eat an' plenty of it. Mammy fixed plenty of dat ham an made lots of bread an' fixed dem coffee. How dey did eat! Dey was jus' as nice as dey could be to Mammy an' when dey wus through dey tole Mammy dat she could have de rest, an' de captain gave her some money an' he tole her dat she wus free, dat we didn' belong to Marse Paul no longer.[213]

West Point on the Eno and the Duke Homestead

During the truce the Union advance line was anchored on the south at Tyrrell's Mount, in Chatham County below Chapel Hill. It ran through the college town to Durham's Station and ended on the north at West Point,[214] a gristmill village on the Eno River—a small Neuse tributary. A Durham city park occupies the village site, and includes the miller's home—the McCown-Mangum House—which, according to local folklore, Kilpatrick's troopers used for target practice with their new repeating rifles while camped on a hillside nearby, presently a shopping center parking lot on U.S. 501 in the

Union soldiers, who were camped at West Point on the Eno River, used the McCown-Mangum House for target practice with their new repeating rifles.

northern part of Durham. A reconstructed mill and a tobacco barn devoted to the work of turn-of-the-twentieth-century photographer Hugh Mangum also stand in the park, which is reached from Stagville by taking the Old Oxford Highway back to town and turning right onto Roxboro Road.

In the same part of Durham there is the 1852 homeplace of Washington Duke, a small farmer reluctantly drafted into the Confederate navy, who came home from a Yankee prison to find his farm stripped except for a small amount of tobacco and, the story goes, a blind mule. Duke went on the road to peddle his tobacco, made enough money to plant another crop and went on to start a leaf manufacturing business that, by 1890, had become the American Tobacco trust controlling ninety percent of the United States's cigarette market. Another state historic site, Duke Homestead is on Duke Homestead Road, just north of I-85 on the way from Stagville and West Point to Bennett Place, where Sherman met Johnston on Monday morning, April 17.

APRIL 17–26—DURHAM

I ordered a car and locomotive to be prepared to convey me up to Durham's at eight o'clock of the morning of April 17th. Just as we were entering the car, the telegraph-operator, whose office was up-stairs in the depot-building,

Sherman and Johnston meet on the road at Bennett farm. *Courtesy of the Bennett Place Historic*

ran down to me and said that he was at that instant of time receiving a most important dispatch in cipher from Morehead City, which I ought to see. I held the train for nearly half an hour, when he returned with the message translated and written out. It was from [Union Secretary of War Edwin] *Stanton, announcing the assassination of Mr. Lincoln, the attempt on the life of* [Secretary of State William Henry] *Seward and son, and a suspicion that a like fate was designed for General Grant and all the principal officers of the Government. Dreading the effect of such a message at that critical instant of time, I asked the operator if any one besides himself had seen it; he answered no. I then bade him not to reveal the contents by word or look till I came back.*[215]

Bennett Place

For a change, the weather was splendid, the air fresh and perfumed with April blossoms. Sherman kept his own counsel, worrying about the effect Lincoln's murder would have when his soldiers learned about it. In fact, rumors to that effect were already running among the troops in Raleigh, "but, it was said, it was 'not credited at Head Quarters,'" and it was not therefore believed by the soldiers.[216] Reaching Durham's Station, Sherman met Kilpatrick and, after a short conference, set out on the Hillsborough

Road with his escort and a trooper with a white flag leading the way. About five miles from the station, they spotted the Confederate party proceeding behind the same standard. The soldiers met, the generals exchanged pleasantries and cast around for a private place to talk. Johnston mentioned a farmhouse he had just passed, and the two men went to ask the hospitality of James and Nancy Bennitt.

Nineteen years later, a journalist named Hiram Paul set out to write a history of what had become the incorporated town of Durham, with a population of more than two thousand. "Anxious to visit this historic spot," Paul set out for the surrender site with tobacco dealer Thomas Decatur Jones and C.B. Green, editor of the town's newspaper, the *Tobacco Plant*, "for the purpose of taking the affidavit of a daughter of old man Bennett." (Why or when the spelling changed is unknown.) They found the house "a plain, old-fashioned, unpretending structure, devoid of paint without and within, but neatness and a certain degree of rustic taste was manifest." They found there a Bennett granddaughter who knew little about the generals' meeting, but she directed them to her aunt Eliza, who lived nearby.

Eliza Bennett Duke Christopher told historian Hiram Paul about the generals' meeting at her parents' farm. *Courtesy of the Bennett Place Historic Site.*

She then, in her own plain way, told us how she stood and saw the two officers, Sherman and Johnston, meet at the gate, shake hands and walk side by side into the house, talking earnestly all the while, and how strange it looked to her to see these two men, who had been fighting each other for four years, meet so friendly and act so gentlemanly toward each other. She said they would frequently come out of the house and take short walks together, and she also said she saw them take a drink from the very bottle, in company with her father, that Mr. T.D. Jones now has in his possession…Going to a book-case in the corner she took from between the leaves of an old book a dilapidated page from Harper's Weekly, dated May 27th, 1865, that contained a perfect representation of the exterior of the Bennett House, as well as the interior of the room that was occupied by the two officers, these gentlemen being seated at a table surrounded with papers, writing materials &c.[217]

After the Bennetts had left Sherman and Johnston alone, Sherman brought out the telegram and let Johnston see it. "The perspiration came out in large drops on his forehead, and he did not attempt to conceal his distress."[218] The generals, though, found they agreed on many points and Johnston, showing the disregard for Davis that would eventually bring him and Sherman to agreement, suggested that, rather than merely settling on the cease-fire to which the Confederate president had agreed so the governments could confer, he and Sherman end the war themselves, on

Johnston and Sherman talk inside Bennetts' cabin. *Courtesy of the Bennett Place Historic Site.*

terms similar to the lenient ones Grant had given Lee. Sherman assured Johnston that he had understood Lincoln's intention to deal easily with the South, but questioned whether Johnston had authority over all Confederate forces or just those in the Carolinas, Georgia and Florida. They agreed to continue the conversation the next day, and retired to their respective bases.[219]

Back in Raleigh, Sherman broke the Lincoln news. "I watched the effect closely, and was gratified that there was no single act of retaliation," he later wrote, "though I saw and felt that one single word by me would have laid the city in ashes, and turned its whole population houseless upon the country, if not worse." Sherman was also busy conferring with his officers, "every one of whom urged me to conclude terms. All dreaded the weary and laborious march after a fugitive and dissolving army."[220] He met Johnston at the Bennett house again on Tuesday, joined this time by Breckinridge, and concluded terms for Johnston's surrender and an armistice to allow their governments to agree to go along. For Sherman's and Johnston's armies, the

The table and bottle that the generals are supposed to have used at Bennett Place. *From Boyd, Story of Durham.*

134

only marching left was on the way home—but no one knew that, and there was waiting left to do.

To reach Bennett Place, get on Interstate 85 in Durham, going west toward Greensboro, then take the U.S. 15-501 exit toward Chapel Hill and immediately exit onto Hillsborough Road. Turn right (west) at the top of the ramp, go through one stoplight, straight where U.S. 70 veers off to the right and under a railroad bridge. The street ends at a *T* intersection with Morreene Road. Turn right, pass McMannen United Methodist Church, cross a railroad track and come to Bennett Memorial Road. The historic site is on your left, enclosed by a low stone wall, with a Civil War Trails kiosk on the left.

Bennett Place State Historic Site consists of a reconstructed farmstead, visitor center with museum and orientation theater and nature trails. A small Bennett family cemetery, cleared of overgrowth in the fall of 2007, stands about two hundred yards east of the site and just off Bennett Memorial Road.

Sherman may have been accurate in reading Lincoln's intentions toward the South, but with the president's death the political mood in Washington had changed. When the terms of his tentative agreement with Johnston

Union troops help themselves to James Bennett's hay while officers converse. *Courtesy of the Bennett Place Historic Site.*

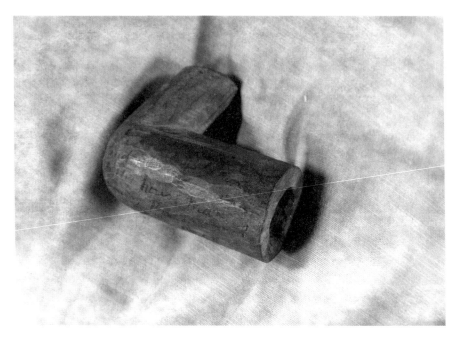

A "Peace pipe" carved from a tree at Bennett Place. *Courtesy of the North Carolina State*

reached the capital, Sherman went from being a national hero to being called a traitor. True enough, Sherman had taken a drink before writing out the terms (neglecting, in his preoccupation, to offer the bottle to Breckinridge, who later called Sherman a "hog" for the lapse of courtesy). But they were in line with what he thought Lincoln would have wanted and the agreement signed at Appomattox: Confederate armies were to be disbanded, soldiers to swear oaths of loyalty, the United States to recognize Southern state governments and Southern citizens' civil rights to be respected.

While the new president, Andrew Johnson (a Raleigh native), Stanton and other officials called Sherman names, the Union and Confederate armies in North Carolina sat idle.

> *The "boys in blue and gray" met in friendly intercourse—swapped horses, ran foot races, shot at targets, and, around the same camp-fires, told hairbreadth escapes, spun camp yarns, and had a "good time" generally.*[221]

Bumming continued in the countryside and in the Durham's Station village, where a number of soldiers—blue, gray or both, depending upon who tells the tale—liberated a stock of tobacco from the "manufactory" of one John Ruffin Green, which stood across the street from the depot. Green figured he was ruined. However, Green concocted his Spanish Flavored Durham Tobacco to appeal to the sophisticated taste of young gentlemen— particularly those of the college in Chapel Hill, who, gone to war, shared it around their Confederate camps. Free samples of the brightleaf blend also made a hit with the Northerners, and soon after hostilities ended and the boys went home, the local post office was flooded with paying orders for more. Green's future was secured, especially after he applied a bull's head logo to his product—origin of the Bull Durham brand that, at the hands of Green's corporate successors, W.T. Blackwell and Julian Shakespeare Carr, became an international favorite within the next fifteen years.[222]

There being still no news of results in the matter pending between Sherman and Johnston, and it being a question in which the humblest and the greatest had an equal interest, the troops again began to murmur. "How long," it was petulantly and perhaps pertinently asked, "does it take a rebel General to surrender?" The dissatisfaction would have been much more marked, had not the matter been in the hands of Gen. Sherman, who, up to that time, among the soldiers I think, was the most popular man in the United States. But when the troops began to suspect that this great commander had assumed, with the duty of restoring the authority of

Captured Confederate supplies in Greensboro. *Courtesy of the North Carolina State Archives.*

the government, the gratuitous job of preserving the self-respect of traitors, they seemed to admire more moderately. Then word came, that the terms of surrender extended to Johnston by Gen. Sherman, were unsatisfactory to the Authorities at Washington, and that Gen. Grant was on his way to Raleigh.[223]

Grant made his surprise appearance on April 24, and directed Sherman to let Johnston know their truce would expire in forty-eight hours. Sherman fired off angry letters in response, to Grant and Stanton, but there was nothing he could do to change minds, especially in so short a time. Johnston wrote back, asking to meet on the twenty-sixth. Again, they arrived at the Bennett farm, and Sherman laid down the law: Johnston's command was to cease all acts of war, deliver its weapons to the Union army at Greensboro and all military personnel to take oaths of allegiance to the United States; officers could keep their sidearms, baggage and horses, and everyone was allowed safe passage home.[224]

Johnston had only practical authority to surrender. Davis, and some of Johnston's officers, wanted to carry on the fight—breaking up the army into guerilla bands to harass a Union occupation. Davis, receiving word of Sherman's ultimatum in Charlotte, ordered Johnston to temporarily scatter

Surrendered Confederates take the Union loyalty oath in Greensboro. *Courtesy of the North Carolina State Archives.*

his men to reassemble later at a location to be determined, and to form a cavalry escort for Davis's continued flight. Johnston was well aware that such behavior could prolong the conflict indefinitely, perhaps for years, and that the army and Southern population were sick and tired of the war. Again flaunting Davis's imagined authority Johnston made peace then and there for the Carolinas, Georgia and Florida. It was the Confederacy's largest surrender, deactivating about eighty thousand troops in all, and leaving only small commands in the field farther west, which shortly capitulated as well.[225]

Johnston and Sherman parted with a great deal of mutual respect and affection. Both men took up their pens to tell their sides of the war and surrender stories, and defend their reputations. Johnston died in 1891 from a cold contracted while serving as one of Sherman's pallbearers. Despite his attempted generosity toward Johnston's army, and his personal affection for the South, Sherman's name became practically a curse in the South, an image in large part passed to posterity by the women who experienced his march firsthand while their menfolk were off being soldiers.[226]

Though long ignored by conventional chroniclers, who stopped paying attention at Appomattox, the Bennett Place surrender, for most practical purposes, ended the War Between the States—as a military conflict, if not

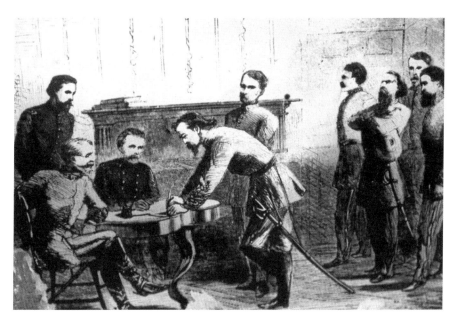

Confederate officers sign their paroles in Greensboro. *Courtesy of the North Carolina State Archives.*

James Bennett at his home after the soldiers had left. *Courtesy of the Durham Public Library.*

one in social, economic and symbolic terms. And it is the final stop on this tour itinerary. The farm, though, went on to have a history of its own.

James and Nancy Bennett lived out their lives on the farm. He died in the 1870s, and she followed a few years later. Eliza, the Bennett daughter whom Hiram Paul interviewed in the 1880s, was the war widow of Robert Duke, a brother of the tobacco man Washington. (She remarried after the war. When Paul met her, she was Eliza Christopher.) In 1890, Washington Duke's eldest son, Brodie—a successful tobacco manufacturer and real estate developer in Durham despite a weakness for liquor, women and commodities markets—bought the property, correctly figuring that it had historic significance, and offered the house for sale at the Chicago Exposition of 1893. Finding no takers, Brodie sold the farm to Samuel Morgan, of a Durham County farming family, who meant to make a historic site of it but died before he could accomplish that purpose.

In 1921, a fire destroyed the house, but Morgan's idea of a memorial at the surrender site had caught on. Attorney R.O. Everett led the effort, along with Frank L. Fuller, a fellow state legislator, and obtained a state commitment of money to keep up the site if the Morgan family would donate the land and chip in for a suitable monument. All agreed and the site acquired a marker of two columns, representing the South and the North, topped by a lintel inscribed with the word "Unity."

R.O. Everett, Durham attorney, led the effort for a memorial at Bennett Place in the 1920s. *Courtesy of the Bennett Place State Historic Site.*

Despite objections from the United Daughters of the Confederacy, who disapproved of a monument to defeat or at least to its ceremonious erection, the Unity marker went up and was dedicated in November 1923 before a crowd of local dignitaries and war veterans. Julian Shakespeare Carr, the Bull Durham magnate, presided. Rich and prominent, he by then went by the honorific "General," though he had mustered out at Appomattox as a cavalry private. The Bennett farmstead was rebuilt for the Civil War centennial of the early 1960s, and became an official state historic site during the local history revival of the 1976 Bicentennial of the Declaration of Independence. Each April, reenactment festivities there commemorate the peace.[227]

Above: Unity monument dedication, November 1923. *Courtesy of the Durham Public Library.*

Left: The Unity monument and the rebuilt Bennett farm buildings.

Sherman's Trail— A Suggested Itinerary

Waxhaw, North Carolina—**Museum of the Waxhaws**
To **Wilson's Store** skirmish memorial, via N.C. 75, Old Monroe Road, Bigham Road
To **Monroe town square**, via N.C. 200
To **Morven**, via U.S. 74/601, White's Store Road, Sandy Ridge Church Road
To **Old Sneedsboro**, via U.S. 52, Sneedsboro Road
To downtown **Wadesborough,** via U.S. 52
To **Laurel Hill**, via U.S. 74
To **Old Laurel Hill Presbyterian Church**, via Old Wire Road
To **Temperance Hall**, via Old Wire Road
To Aberdeen—**Malcolm Blue Farm**, via U.S. 15–501, N.C. 5
To **Rockfish**, via N.C. 211, U.S. 401, Rockfish Road
To Fayetteville—**Cape Fear Museum/Arsenal Park**, via U.S. 401
To **Cross Creek Cemetery**, via Grove Street, Cool Springs Street
To **Averasboro Battlefield**, via U.S. 301, N.C. 82 (Burnett Road)
To **Bentonville Battlefield**, via U.S. 301, N.C. 55, U.S. 701, Harper House Road
To Goldsboro, **Wayne County Museum**, via Harper House Road, N.C. 581, Ash Street, William Street
To **Smithfield**, via Harper House Road, Devil's Racetrack Road, U.S. 301
To Raleigh—**Capitol Square**, via U.S. 70, N.C. 210, I-40, South Saunders Street
To **Oakwood Cemetery**, via Morgan Street, Person Street, Oakwood Avenue
To **Raleigh National Cemetery**, via Oakwood Avenue, Tarboro Road (Rock Quarry Road)

To Danville, Virginia—**Museum of Fine Arts and History**, via U.S. 70, N.C. 147, I-85, N.C. 86, South Main Street

To Greensboro, North Carolina—**Historical Museum**, via U.S. 29, Summit Avenue

To Hillsborough—**Dickson House**, via I-85, U.S. 70, Churton Street, King Street

To **Morrisville**, via I-85, N.C. 147, I-40, Aviation Parkway

To Durham—**Leigh Farm**, via I-40, N.C. 54, Leigh Farm Road

To **Stagville**, via I-40, U.S. 15-501, I-85, Red Mill Road, Old Oxford Highway

To **West Point on the Eno**, via Old Oxford Highway, Roxboro Street

To **Duke Homestead**, via Roxboro Street, Duke Street, Carver Street, Duke Homestead Road

To **Bennett Place**, via Guess Road, I-85, Hillsborough Road, Bennett Memorial Road

Useful Names and Numbers

(Times change. Check ahead.)

Museum of the Waxhaws
8215 Waxhaw Highway (N.C. 75 East)
Waxhaw, NC 28173
Hours: Friday and Saturday, 10:00 a.m.–5:00 p.m.; Sunday, 2:00–5:00 p.m.
(704) 843-1832
http://www.perigee.net/~mwaxhaw
Admission: Adults, $4.00 Children (6–12), $2.

Old Laurel Hill Presbyterian Church
15301 McFarland Road
Laurinburg, NC 28352
Office hours: weekday mornings, but call ahead
(910) 276-7151
http://laurelhillpc.org

Malcolm Blue Farm Museum
1177 Bethesda Road (Highway 5 South & E.L. Ives Drive)
Aberdeen, NC 28315
Hours: Wednesday through Saturday, 11:00 a.m.–2:00 p.m.
(910) 944-7558
http://malcolmbluefarm.com

Museum of the Cape Fear Historical Complex
801 Arsenal Avenue
Fayetteville, NC 28305
Hours: Tuesday through Saturday, 10:00 a.m.–5:00 p.m.; Sunday, 1:00–5:00 p.m.
(910) 486-1330
http://ncmuseumofhistory.org/osm/mcf.html

Averasboro Battlefield Museum
N.C. 82, three miles east of Erwin
P.O. Box 1811
Dunn, NC 28335-1811
Hours: Tuesday through Saturday, 10:00 a.m.–4:00 p.m.; Sunday, 1:00–4:00 p.m.
(910) 891-5019
http://www.averasboro.com

Bentonville Battlefield
5466 Harper House Road
Four Oaks, NC 27524
Hours: April 1 through October 31
Monday through Saturday, 9:00 a.m.–5:00 p.m.; Sunday 1:00–5:00 p.m.
November 1 through March 31
Tuesday through Saturday 10:00 a.m.–4:00 p.m.; Sunday 1:00–4:00 p.m.
(910) 594-0789
http://www.ah.dcr.state.nc.us/sections/hs/bentonvi/bentonvi.htm

Wayne County Historical Association and Museum
116 N. William Street
P.O. Box 665
Goldsboro, NC 27533-0665
Hours: Tuesday through Friday, 12:00–5:00 p.m. or appointment
(919) 734-5023
http://www.waynecountyhistoricalnc.org

Danville Museum of Fine Arts & History
975 Main Street
Danville, Virginia 24541
Hours: Tuesday through Friday, 10:00 a.m.–5:00 p.m.; Saturday and
    Sunday, 2:00 p.m.–5:00 p.m.
(434) 793-5644
http://www.danvillemuseum.org

Greensboro Historical Museum
130 Summit Avenue
Greensboro, N.C. 27401
Hours: Tuesday through Saturday, 10:00 a.m.–5:00 p.m.; Sunday, 2:00–
    5:00 p.m.
(336) 373-2043
http://www.greensborohistory.org

Alexander Dickson House–Orange County Visitor's Center
150 E. King St.
Hillsborough, NC 27278
Hours: Monday through Friday, 9:00 a.m.–4:00 p.m.; Saturday, 10:00
   a.m.–4:00 p.m.; Sunday 1:00–4:00 p.m.
(919) 732-7741
www.historichillsborough.org

Historic Stagville State Historic Site
5828 Old Oxford Highway
Durham, NC 27712
Hours: Tuesday through Saturday, 10:00 a.m.–4:00 p.m.
(919) 620-0120
http://www.historicstagvillefoundation.org

West Point on the Eno Park
5101 North Roxboro Road
Durham, N.C. 27712
Hours: Gates open daily, 8:00 a.m.–sundown. Historic buildings open
   Saturday and Sunday, 1:00–5:00 p.m. mid-March through mid-
   December
(919) 471-1623
http://www.durhamnc.gov/departments/parks/parks.cfm

Duke Homestead State Historic Site
2828 Duke Homestead Road
Durham, NC 27705
Hours: Tuesday through Saturday 10:00 a.m.–4:00 p.m.
(919) 477-5498
http://www.ah.dcr.state.nc.us/Sections/hs/duke/duke.htm

Bennett Place State Historic Site
4409 Bennett Memorial Rd.
Durham, NC 27705
Hours: Tuesday through Saturday 10:00 a.m.–4:00 p.m.
(919) 383-4345
http://www.ah.dcr.state.nc.us/Sections/hs/bennett/bennett.htm

Notes

CHAPTER ONE: GOLDSBORO, MARCH 23

1. Lloyd Lewis, *Sherman: Fighting Prophet* (New York: Harcourt, Brace and Company, 1932), 509.

2. U.S. War Department, U.S. Records and Pension Office, U.S. War Records Office et al, *The War of Rebellion: A Compilation of the Official Records of the Union and Confederate Armies* Series I, Vol. XLVII, Part II (Washington: Government Print Office, 1895), 719 (hereafter cited as *Official Records*).

3. *Hillsborough Recorder*, March 22, 1865, 2.

4. George W. Nichols, *The Story of the Great March: From the Diary of a Staff-Officer* (New York: Harper & Brothers, 1865), 253.

5. Thomas W. Osborn, *The Fiery Trail: A Union Officer's Account of Sherman's Last Campaigns* (Knoxville: The University of Tennessee Press, 1986), 202–3.

6. Nichols, *The Story*, 275–6.

7. *Official Records*, Series I, Vol. XLVII, Part I, 1057.

8. William T. Sherman, *Memoirs of General W.T. Sherman* (New York: Library of America, 1990), 205–224.

9. *Official Records*, Series I, Vol. XLVII, Part II, 1247.

10. Joseph E. Johnston, *Narrative of Military Operations Directed, During the Late War Between the States* (New York: D. Appleton and Company, 1874), 392–3.

11. Nichols, *The Story*, 266.

12. Wilson Angley, Jerry L. Cross, and Michael Hill, *Sherman's March Through North Carolina: A Chronology* (Raleigh: North Carolina Division of Archives and History, 1995), 45.

13. Arthur Peronneau Ford, *Life in the Confederate Army: Being Personal Experiences of a Private Soldier in the Confederate Army* (New York and Washington, DC: Neale Publishing Company, 1905), 63.

14. *Hillsborough Recorder*, March 22, 1865, 3.

15. Ibid.

16. Elizabeth Waties Allston Pringle, *Chronicles of Chicora Wood* (Georgetown County Historical Society, 1999), 241.

17. Osborn, *Fiery Trail*, 516–7.

Chapter Two: Moving In

18. General Joe Wheeler Foundation, "Joseph Wheeler," http://www.wheelerplantation.org/Joe.htm.

19. Arlington National Cemetery, "Joseph Wheeler," http://www.arlingtoncemetery.net/jwheeler.htm.

20. *Official Records*, Series I, Vol. XLVII, Part II, 154–6.

21. Lewis, *Sherman*, 432.

22. Brooks D. Simpson and Jean V. Berlin, *Sherman's Civil War: Selected Correspondence of William T. Sherman, 1860–1865* (Chapel Hill: University of North Carolina Press, 1999), 762.

23. *Hillsborough Recorder*, March 1, 1865, 2.

24. *Official Records*, Series I, Vol. XLVII, Part II, 1222.

25. Ibid., Part I, 865.

26. Ibid., Part II, 593.

27. Lewis, *Sherman*, 404.

28. James Reston, *Sherman's March and Vietnam* (New York: MacMillan, 1984), 145.

29. *Official Records*, Series I, Vol. I, 859. The "well-timed interview" refers to information brought back by one of Kilpatrick's officers who met Confederate pickets under a flag of truce while conveying a message between Sherman and the Southern General Wade Hampton.

30. *Official Records*, Series I, Vol. XLVII, Part II, 602–3.

31. Ibid., 603.

32. Diane Wilson, "Real Skirmish Lends Authenticity," *The Enquirer-Journal*, September 16, 1983, 2A.

33. Louise Pettus, "Belk Retail Empire Sprang from Lancaster County," *Charlotte Observer*, July 28, 2002, 8Y.

34. *Official Records*, Series I, Vol. XLVII, Part I, 867. Reference is to the "Battle of Waxhaws" or "Buford's Massacre," May 29, 1780.

35. Ibid., Part II, 1122–3.

36. Ibid., Part I, 4; Part II, 1130.

37. Gene Stowe, "Reviving a Piece of History," *Charlotte Observer*, 1983; Ralph P. Ganis, "Sherman's Feint Toward Charlotte," unpublished paper given to the author by Julie Ganis, 2001.

38. Ralph P. Ganis, "Skirmish at Wilson's Store" in Virginia A.S.K. Bjorlin, ed., *The Heritage of Union County*, Vol. II (Monroe, NC: Carolinas Genealogical Society, 1993), 70–71.

39. H. Nelson Walden, *History of Union County* (Monroe, NC: Self-published, 1964), 17.

40. *Official Records*, Series I, Vol. XLVII, Part II, 1301.

41. Ibid., Part II, 1122.

42. Ibid., 652.

43. Virginia A.S. Kendrick, *Looking Back at Monroe's History* (Monroe, NC: City of Monroe, 1995), 6.

44. Bjorlin, *Heritage*, 20; Walden, *History*, 15.

45. "A Wagon Train Once Camped on the Public Square," *Monroe Journal*, June 28, 1910, http://freepages.genealogy.rootsweb.com/~jganis/unionco/CivilWarUnionCounty2.html (accessed Oct. 20, 2007).

46. *Hillsborough Recorder*, March 29, 1865, 1.

47. Ibid., March 1, 1865, 2.

48. Angley et al., *Sherman's March*, 3.

49. Jacqueline Glass Campbell, *When Sherman Marched North From the Sea: Resistance on the Confederate Home Front* (Chapel Hill: University of North Carolina Press, 2003), 83–84.

50. Lewis, *Sherman*, 511.

51. Mary L. Medley, *History of Anson County, North Carolina 1750–1976* (Wadesboro, NC: Anson County Historical Society, 1976), 111.

52. Marshall Delancey Haywood, *Lives of the Bishops of North Carolina* (Raleigh, NC: Alfred Williams & Company, 1910), xx.

53. Sherman, *Memoirs*, 772.

54. *Official Records*, Series I, Vol. XLVII, Part II, 671.

55. *North Carolina Argus* (Wadesboro), March 30, 1865.

56. Medley, *History*, 11; Anson County Chamber of Commerce, http://www.ansoncounty.org/aboutanson.html.

57. Medley, *History*, 670.

58. Ibid., 893–4.

59. Ibid., 689.

60. Ibid., 118.

61. *North Carolina Argus* (Wadesboro), March 30, 1865.

62. Joseph Blount Cheshire, *The Church in the Confederate States: A History of the Protestant Episcopal Church in the Confederate States* (New York, London, Bombay and Calcutta: Longmans, Green and Co., 1912), appendix.

63. Larry Tise, "Thomas Atkinson, 6 Aug. 1807–4 Jan. 1881" in *Dictionary of North Carolina Biography* (Chapel Hill: University of North Carolina Press, 1979–1996), 62–3.

64. Cornelia Phillips Spencer, *The Last Ninety Days of the War in North-Carolina* (New York: Watchman Publishing Company, 1866), 62–3.

65. Ibid., 671; John Dunlap, in conversation with the author, September 2007.

66. *Official Records*, Series I, Vol. XLVII, Part I, 885–6.

67. Ibid., 689.

68. Spencer, *Last Ninety Days*, 63–4.

69. *North Carolina Argus* (Wadesboro), March 30, 1865.

70. Margaret E. Rush, letter to *Arkansas Gazette*, Oct. 6, 1907, http://www.rootsweb.com/~ncanson/military/raiders.htm.

71. *North Carolina Argus* (Wadesboro), March 30, 1865.

72. Medley, *History*, 122–3.

73. John Hutchinson, *No Ordinary Lives: A History of Richmond County, North Carolina 1750–1900* (Virginia Beach, VA: Donning Company Publishers, 1998), 137–9.

74. *Official Records*, Series I, Vol. XLVII, Part II, 904.

75. Hutchinson, *No Ordinary*, 143.

76. *Official Records*, Series I, Vol. XLVII, Part I, 690, 861.

77. Ibid., Part II, 721.

78. Sherman, *Memoirs*, 774.

79. Craig L. Symonds, *Joseph E. Johnston: A Civil War Biography* (New York: W.W. Norton and Company, 1992), 340.

80. Johnston, *Narrative*, 371.

81. Joe DePriest, "Scent of Apple Pie Is a Powerful Lure," *Charlotte Observer*, September 15, 2006.

82. Symonds, *Johnston*, 342–3.

83. Johnston, *Narrative*, 371.

84. Symonds, *Johnston*, 344; Johnston, *Narrative*, 372.

85. Johnston, *Narrative*, 372–8.

86. *Official Records*, Series I, Vol. XLVII, Part I, 690.

87. Ibid., Part II, 1345; John G. Barrett, *The Civil War in North Carolina* (Chapel Hill: University of North Carolina Press, 1963), 122 n. 29.

88. Barrett, *The Civil War*, 302.

89. Ibid., 363–4.

90. Edwin E. Bryant, *The Third Regiment of Wisconsin Veteran Volunteer Infantry 1861–1865* (Madison, WI: Veteran Association of the Regiment, 1891), 313–4.

91. Lewis, *Sherman*, 509.

92. Nichols, *The Story*, 217–8.

93. Dick Brown, "Sherman Closed Tar Heel Business," *The News and Observer*, July 26, 1953, 6-VI.

94. G.F. Kirkpatrick, "A Brief History of Laurel Hill Presbyterian Church 1797–1947," http://www.rootsweb.com/~ncrichmo/oldlaurel.html; Reverend Howard H. Whitehurst, interview by author, September 26, 2007.

95. Sylvia McRae McLean, "Old Laurel Hill Presbyterian Church," http://laurelhillpc.org/index.php?page=history.

96. Sherman, *Memoirs*, 775.

97. Nichols, *The Story*, 222–3.

98. Betty P. Myers, "Scotland County North Carolina," http://www.scotlandcounty.org/History.htm.

99. Barrett, *The Civil War*, 302.

100. *Official Records*, Series I, Vol. XLVII, Part II, 1332–5.

Chapter Three: Fighting Through

101. Malcolm Blue Historical Society, http://malcolmbluefarm.com.

102. *Official Records*, Series I, Vol. XLVII, Part II, 1347–8.

103. Ibid., Part I, 861.

104. Ibid., Part I, 786, 861.

105. Posey Hamilton, "The Effort to Capture Kilpatrick," *Confederate Veteran* 29: 9 (September 1921): 329; H.H. Scott, "'Fighting' Kilpatrick's Escape," *Confederate Veteran* 12:12 (December 1904): 588; John G. Barrett, *Sherman's March Through the Carolinas* (Chapel Hill: University of North Carolina Press, 1956), 127–8.

106. John A. McGeachy, "In Sherman's Wake: Refugees of the March Through the Carolinas," http://www4.ncsu.edu/~jam3/sherman.htm.

107. *Official Records*, Series I, Vol. XLVII, Part I, 861; Barrett, *Sherman's March*, 128.

108. *Official Records*, Series I, Vol. XLVII, Part I, 1130.

109. Ibid., 862.

110. Steve Ross, "History of the 1st Alabama Cavalry, US Volunteers," www.1stalabamacavalryusv.com.

111. Nichols, *The Story*, 225–30.

112. *Official Records*, Series I, Vol. XLVII, Part I, 382.

113. Ibid., Part II, 762–3.

114. Ibid., 764.

115. Ibid., 763.

116. Katharine M. Jones, *When Sherman Came: Southern Women and the "Great March"* (New York: The Bobbs-Merrill Co., 1964), 264.

117. *Recorder*, March 15, 1865.

118. *Richmond Examiner*, March 10, 1865. Quoted in *Official Records*, Series I, Vol. XLVII, Part II, 753.

119. *Official Records*, Series I, Vol. XLVII, Part II, 1334.

120. Daniel W. Barefoot, *General Robert F. Hoke: Lee's Modest Warrior* (Winston-Salem, NC: John F. Blair Publisher, 2001), 283.

121. Ibid., 291.

122. Aubrey Lee Brooks and Hugh Talmadge Lefler, eds., *The Papers of Walter Clark*, Vol. I, *1857–1901* (Chapel Hill, NC: University of North Carolina Press, 1948), 49–52.

123. Barefoot, *General Robert*, 290–1.

124. Angley et al., *Sherman's March*, 17–19.

125. *Recorder*, March 15, 1865, 2.

126. Josephine Bryan Worth, "Sherman's Raid" in *War Days in Fayetteville* (Fayetteville, NC: J.E.B. Stuart Chapter, United Daughters of the Confederacy, 1910), 47–8.

127. Barrett, *Sherman's March*, 132–3; *Official Records*, Series I, Vol. XLVII, Part I, 204; Worth, "Sherman's Raid," 49.

128. Eliza Tillinghast Stinson, "The Taking of the Arsenal," in *War Days*, 9–10.

129. Sherman, *Memoirs*, 776.

130. Lewis, *Sherman*, 514; Barrett, *Sherman's March*, 140.

131. Lewis, *Sherman*, 1–2.

132. William Wirt Calkins, *The History of the One Hundredth and Fourth Regiment of Illinois Volunteer Infantry: War of the Great Rebellion 1862–1865* (Chicago: Donohue & Henneberry, 1895), 296.

133. Nichols, *The Story*, 236.

134. Osborn, *Fiery Trail*, 178.

135. M.A. DeWolfe Howe, ed., *Marching With Sherman: Passages From the Letters and Campaign Diaries of Henry Hitchcock, Major and Adjutant General of Volunteers November 1864–May 1865* (New Haven, CT: Yale University Press, 1927), 263, 267.

136. Ford, *Life*, 42–43.

137. Sherman, *Memoirs*, 779.

138. Worth, "Sherman's Raid," 51–2.

139. Barrett, *Sherman's March*, 141.

140. *Official Records*, Series I, Vol. XLVII, Part II, 704.

141. *Recorder*, April 5, 1865, 2–3.

142. Barrett, *Sherman's March*, 143–4.

143. Worth, "Sherman's Raid," 52–3.

144. F.Y. Hedley, *Marching Through Georgia: Pen-Pictures of Every-Day Life in General Sherman's Army, From the Beginning of the Atlanta Campaign Until the Close of the War* (Chicago: M.A. Donohue & Co., 1884), 401.

145. Sherman, *Memoirs*, 777–80.

146. Simpson and Berlin, *Sherman's Civil War*, 823–4.

147. Hedley, *Marching*, 404–5.

148. *Recorder*, March 22, 1865, 2.

149. *Official Records*, Series I, Vol. XLVII, Part II, 800.

150. Barrett, *Sherman's March*, 148–9.

151. *Official Records*, Series I, Vol. XLVII, Part I, 1084; Barrett, *Sherman's March*, 150; Averasboro Battlefield Commission, http://www.averasboro.com.

152. Sherman, *Memoirs*, 783.

153. Howe, *Marching*, 289.

154. Edwin E. Bryant, *History of the Third Regiment of Wisconsin Veteran Volunteer Infantry* (Madison, WI: The Veteran Association of the Regiment, 1893), 316.

155. Matthew H. Jamison, *Recollections of Pioneer and Army Life* (Kansas City, KS: Hudson Press, 1911), 320.

156. Averasboro Commission.

157. Averasboro Commission, "Averasboro Advocate: A Preservation Newsletter," Spring 1995, 2.

158. Averasboro Commission Website.

159. North Carolina Historic Sites, "Bentonville Battlefield." http://www.ah.dcr.state.nc.us/sections/hs/bentonvi/bentonvi.htm.

160. Sherman, *Memoirs*, 784–5.

161. Sherman, *Memoirs*, 785.

162. *Official Records*, Series I, Vol. XLVII, Part II, 1427–36.

163. Barrett, *Sherman's March*, 162–5.

164. Sherman, *Memoirs*, 785.

165. Calkins, *The History*, 297–8.

166. Bryant, *History*, 322.

167. Ford, *Life*, 54.

168. Symonds, *Johnston*, 350; Aubrey Lee Brooks, and Hugh Talmadge Lefler, eds., *The Papers of Walter Clark*. Vol. I, *1857–1901* (Chapel Hill: University of North Carolina Press, 1948), 136.

169. Symonds, *Johnston*, 350–1; Barefoot, *General Roberts*, 298; Calkins, *The History*, 305.

170. Jamison, *Recollections*, 321; Hedley, *Marching*, 406; Angley et al., *Sherman's March*, 40; Brooks and Lefler, *Clark Papers*, 136.

171. North Carolina Civil War Tourism Council, "Battle of Bentonville: A First Person Recounting," *The Watch Fire*, February 1999, 1–2; Thad Stem Jr., "10-Year-Old Girl Who Crawled Past Sherman's Line Sees The Civil War Again—This Time In a Safer Way," *Durham Morning Herald*, May 5, 1940, II-1.

172. *Official Records*, Series I, Vol. XLVII, Part I, 1131.

173. J.A. Mowris, *A History of the One Hundred and Seventeenth Regiment, N.Y. Volunteers (Fourth Oneida), From the Date of Its Organization, August 1862, Till That of Its Muster Out, June 1865* (Hartford, CT: Case, Lockwood and Company, Printers, 1866), 192, 200.

174. Osborn, *Fiery Trail*, 199.

175. Bryant, *History*, 326.

176. Ford, *Life*, 54.

CHAPTER FOUR: WRAPPING UP

177. Wayne County Public Library, http://www.wcpl.org/waynesborough.htm; Lynn Setzer, "New Life for Old Waynesboro," *News & Observer* (Raleigh, NC), February 14, 2002, E2; Jim Wise, "Railroad, Spiked Well help form village," *The Herald-Sun* (Durham, NC), January 14, 2001, H1.

178. Hedley, *Marching*, 326; Jamison, *Recollections*, 323.

179. Simpson and Berlin, *Sherman's Civil War*, 827–8. Later, before leaving Goldsboro, Sherman did send his wife the Confederate flag taken from the South Carolina statehouse, but not without fretting over the propriety of a general's family possessing captured goods as souvenirs.

180. Sherman, *Memoirs*, 789.

181. Howe, *Marching*, 273–4.

182. Osborn, *Fiery Trail*, 205.

183. Sherman, *Memoirs*, 813.

184. Johnston, *Narrative*, 394.

185. Ridley, Bromfield Lewis, *Battles and Sketches of the Army of Tennessee* (Mexico: Missouri Printing and Publishing Co., 1906), 453–4.

186. Brooks and Lefler, *Clark Papers*, 136.

187. Mowris, *A History*, 209.

188. *Official Records*, Series I, Vol. XLVII, Part II, p. 1150.

189. Ibid., 1449–60; Angley et al., *Sherman's March*, 48–53; Symonds, *Johnston*, 352–3.

190. Brooks and Lefler, *Clark Papers*, 138.

191. Ibid., 137.

192. Ridley, *Battles*, 456.

193. Caswell County Historical Association, http://www.rootsweb.com/~ncccha/index.html.

194. Ford, *Life*, 63.

195. Ridley, *Battles*, 457.

196. Symonds, *Johnston*, 354.

197. Howe, *Marching*, 285.

198. Nichols, *The Story*, 291–2.

199. Jamison, *Recollections*, 326.

200. Bryant, *History*, 329.

201. Mowris, *A History*, 200.

202. Angley et al., *Sherman's March*, 66; Barrett, *Sherman's March*, 210–7.

203. Symonds, *Johnston*, 355.

204. *Official Records*, Series I, Vol. XLVII, Part I, 31; Calkins, *The History*, 312.

205. Mowris, *A History*, 210–1.

206. Nichols, *The Story*, 299.

207. *Official Records*, Series I, Vol. XLVII, Part III, 198.

208. *Recorder*, April 5, 1865, 2–3.

209. Ernest Dollar, "The Battle of Morrisville," http://www.mindspring.com/~nixnox/history2.html.

210. Sherman, *Memoirs*, 835.

211. Dollar, "Morrisville."

212. Jim Wise, "Old Times in New Hope," *The Herald-Sun* (Durham, NC), September 12, 2000, E1.

213. Jean Bradley Anderson, *Piedmont Plantation* (Durham, NC: Historic Preservation Society of Durham, 1985), 117.

214. *Official Records*, Series I, Vol. XLVII, Part III, 250.

215. Sherman, *Memoirs*, 836.

216. Mowris, *A History*, 211.

217. Hiram V. Paul, *History of the Town of Durham, N.C.* (Raleigh: Edwards, Broughton & Co., 1884), xii–xvi.

218. Sherman, *Memoirs*, 837.

219. Ibid., 837–8; Lewis, *Sherman*, 535–6; Symonds, *Johnston*, 356.

220. Sherman, *Memoirs*, 839; *Official Records*, Series I, Vol. XLVII, Part I, p. 33.

221. Paul, *History*, 25.

222. Nannie M. Tilley, *The Bright-Tobacco Industry, 1860–1929* (Chapel Hill: University of North Carolina Press, 1948), 548.

223. Mowris, *A History*, 212.

224. Sherman, *Memoirs*, 848–51.

225. Barrett, *Sherman's March*, 268–9. For a full and fascinating treatment of the Appomattox and Bennett Place surrenders and the individuals involved, see Jay Winik, *April 1865: The Month That Saved America* (New York: HarperCollins Publishers Inc., 2001).

226. See Campbell, Jones and J. Michael Martinez, William D. Richardson and Ron McNinch-Su, eds., *Confederate Symbols in the Contemporary South* (Gainesville: University Press of Florida, 2000).

227. Jean Bradley Anderson, *Durham County: A History of Durham County, North Carolina* (Durham, NC: Duke University Press in association with The Historic Preservation Society of Durham, 1990), 126, 326–7.

Bibliography

Anderson, Jean Bradley. *Durham County*. Durham, NC: Duke University Press in association with the Historic Preservation Society of Durham, 1990.

———. *Piedmont Plantation: The Bennehan-Cameron Family and Lands in North Carolina*. Durham, NC: Historic Preservation Society of Durham, 1985.

Angley, Wilson, Jerry L. Cross, and Michael Hill. *Sherman's March Through North Carolina: A Chronology*. Raleigh, NC: Division of Archives and History, 1995.

Averasboro Battlefield Commission. http://www.averasboro.com, 2007.

Barefoot, Daniel W. *General Robert F. Hoke: Lee's Modest Warrior*. Winston-Salem, NC: John Blair, 1996.

Barrett, John G. *The Civil War in North Carolina*. Chapel Hill: University of North Carolina Press, 1963.

———. *Sherman's March Through the Carolinas*. Chapel Hill: University of North Carolina Press, 1956.

Barrett, John G., and W. Buck Yearns, eds. *North Carolina Civil War Documentary*. Chapel Hill: University of North Carolina Press, 1980.

Bjorlin, Virginia A.S.K. *The Heritage of Union County, North Carolina*. Monroe, NC: Union County Genealogical Society, 1993.

Bradley, Mark L. *This Astounding Close: The Road to Bennett Place*. Chapel Hill: University of North Carolina Press, 2000.

———. *Last Stand in the Carolinas: The Battle of Bentonville*. Campbell, CA: Savas Woodbury Publishers, 1996.

Brooks, Aubrey Lee, and Hugh Talmadge Lefler, eds. *The Papers of Walter Clark.* Vol. I, *1857–1901.* Chapel Hill: University of North Carolina Press, 1948.

Bryant, Edwin E. *History of the Third Regiment of Wisconsin Veteran Volunteer Infantry, 1861–1865.* Madison, WI: Veterans Association of the Regiment, 1891.

Calkins, William Wirt. *The History of the One Hundred and Fourth Regiment of Illinois Volunteers Infantry: War of the Great Rebellion 1862–1865.* Chicago: Donohue & Henneberry, 1895.

Campbell, Jacqueline Glass. *When Sherman Marched North From the Sea: Resistance on the Confederate Home Front.* Chapel Hill: University of North Carolina Press, 2003.

Cheshire, Joseph Blount. *The Church in the Confederate States: A History of the Protestant Episcopal Church in the Confederate States.* New York: Longmans, Green and Co., 1912.

Dollar, Ernest. *The Battle of Morrisville.* Central North Carolina Historic Preservation. http://www.mindspring.com/~nixnox/index.html, 2006.

Ford, Arthur P. *Life in the Confederate Army: Being Personal Experiences of a Private Soldier in the Confederate Army.* New York and Washington, D.C.: Neale Publishing Company, 1905.

Ganis, Julie Harris. "The Civil War in and Around Union County, North Carolina." http://freepages.genealogy.rootsweb.com/~jganis/unionco/unioncocivilwar.html, 2006.

Ganis, Ralph P. "Sherman's Feint Toward Charlotte (Feb. 17–March 1, 1865)." Draft, 1985.

Hedley, F.Y. *Marching Through Georgia: Pen-Pictures of Every-Day Life In General Sherman's Army, From the Beginning of the Atlanta Campaign Until the Close of the War.* Chicago: M.A. Donohue & Co., 1884.

Hillsborough Recorder, January 4 through April 5, 1865.

Howe, M.A. DeWolfe, ed. *Marching With Sherman: Passages from the Letters and Campaign Diaries of Henry Hitchcock, Major and Adjutant General of Volunteers November 1864– May 1865.* New Haven, CT: Yale University Press, 1927.

Hutchinson, John. *No Ordinary Lives: A History of Richmond County, North Carolina 1750–1900.* Virginia Beach, VA: Donning Company Publishers, 1998.

Jamison, Matthew H. *Recollections of Pioneer and Army Life.* Kansas City, MO: Hudson Press, 1911.

Johnson, Bradley Tyler, ed. *A memoir of the Life and Public Service of Joseph E. Johnston, Once the Quartermaster General of the Army of the United States, and a General in the Army of the Confederate States of America.* Baltimore, MD: R.H. Woodward & Company, 1891.

Johnston, Joseph E. *Narrative of Military Operations Directed, During the Late War Between the States.* New York: D. Appleton, 1874.

Jones, Katharine M. *When Sherman Came: Southern Women and the "Great March.* New York: Bobbs-Merrill, 1964.

Kendrick, Virginia A.S. *Looking Back at Monroe's History.* Monroe, NC: City of Monroe, 1975.

Lewis, Lloyd. *Sherman: Fighting Prophet.* New York: Harcourt, Brace and Company, 1932.

Medley, Mary L. *History of Anson County, North Carolina 1750–1976.* Wadesboro, NC: Anson County Historical Society, 1976.

Meyer, Duane Gilbert. *The Highland Scots of North Carolina 1732–1776.* Chapel Hill: University of North Carolina Press, 1961.

Nichols, George W. *The Story of the Great March: From the Diary of a Staff-Officer.* New York: Harper & Brothers, 1865.

North Carolina Historic Sites. "Bentonville Battlefield." http://www.ah.dcr.state.nc.us/sections/hs/bentonvi/bentonvi.htm, 2007.

Oates, John A. *The Story of Fayetteville and the Upper Cape Fear.* Fayetteville, NC: John A. Oates, 1950.

Osborn, Thomas Ward. *The Fiery Trail: A Union Officer's Account of Sherman's Last Campaigns.* Knoxville: University of Tennessee Press, 1986.

Paul, Hiram V. *History of the Town of Durham, N.C.* Raleigh, NC: Edwards, Broughton & Co., 1884.

Powell, William S. *The North Carolina Gazetteer: A Dictionary of Tar Heel Places.* Chapel Hill: University of North Carolina Press, 1968.

Pringle, Elizabeth Waties Allston. *Chronicles of Chicora Wood.* Georgetown, SC: Georgetown County Historical Society, 1999.

Reston, James. *Sherman's March and Vietnam* New York: MacMillan, 1984.

Ridley, Bromfield Lewis. *Battles and Sketches of the Army of Tennessee.* Mexico: Missouri Printing and Publishing Co., 1906.

Sherman, William T. *Memoirs of General W.T. Sherman.* New York: Library of America, 1990.

Simpson, Brooks D., and Jean V. Berlin, eds. *Sherman's Civil War: Selected Correspondence of William T. Sherman, 1860–1865.* Chapel Hill: University of North Carolina Press, 1999.

Spencer, Cornelia Phillips. *The Last Ninety Days of the War in North-Carolina.* New York: Watchman Publishing Company, 1866.

Symonds, Craig L. *Joseph E. Johnston: A Civil War Biography.* New York: W.W. Norton & Co., 1992.

Walden, H. Nelson. *History of Union County.* Monroe, NC: H. Nelson Walden, 1964.

The War of the Rebellion: A Compilation of the Official Records of the Union and Confederate Armies. Washington, D.C.: Government Printing Office, 1880–1901.

War Days in Fayetteville. Fayetteville, NC: J.E.B. Stuart Chapter, United Daughters of the Confederacy, 1910.

Wilson, Louis R., ed. *Collected Papers of Cornelia Phillips Spencer.* Chapel Hill: University of North Carolina Press, 1953.

Winik, Jay. *April 1865: The Month That Saved America.* New York: HarperCollins Publishers Inc., 2001.

Yetman, Norman R., ed. *Voices From Slavery.* New York: Holt, Rinehart and Winston, 1970.